Grammar Success

1

TEACHER'S GUIDE

Raising Writing Standards

Pie Corbett   Rachel Roberts

OXFORD
UNIVERSITY PRESS

OXFORD
UNIVERSITY PRESS

Great Clarendon Street, Oxford OX2 6DP

Oxford University Press is a department of the University of Oxford.
It furthers the University's objective of excellence in research, scholarship,
and education by publishing worldwide in

Oxford   New York

Auckland   Bangkok   Buenos Aires   Cape Town   Chennai
Dar es Salaam   Delhi   Hong Kong   Istanbul   Karachi   Kolkata
Kuala Lumpur   Madrid   Melbourne   Mexico City   Mumbai   Nairobi
São Paulo   Shanghai   Taipei   Tokyo   Toronto

First published 2000
Reprinted 2003

10 9 8 7 6 5 4 3

British Library Cataloguing in Publication Data

Data available

ISBN 0 19 834289 6

Designed and produced by Oxford Designers & Illustrators Ltd
Printed in Great Britain by Athenæum Press Ltd, Gateshead, Tyne-and-Wear

With thanks to Margaret Cunningham, Anna Aaron, and the children of
Class 3 at Pleasant Street County Primary, Liverpool, for the children's work
featured in this book and on the cover of Grammar Success 1.

Although every effort has been made to trace and contact copyright holders
prior to publication, this has not been possible in every case. If notified, the
publisher undertakes to rectify any errors or omissions at the earliest
opportunity.

Contents

Introduction

Grammar Success is about teaching children how to use grammar to improve their writing. It provides materials, not only to deepen children's understanding, but also to refine their grammatical skills and to enable them to apply these to their own writing.

Teaching grammatical skills

The course helps pupils to understand grammar but also to become skilful in these key grammatical areas:

- **Sentence construction** – the ability to construct, vary, and control a variety of sentence structures.
- **Punctuation** – the ability to use punctuation to indicate to the reader how a text should be read.
- **Language effects** – the ability to enhance writing, using words powerfully and effectively, plus handling such effects as *simile*, *metaphor*, and *alliteration*.
- **Cohesion** – creating cohesive links within and between sentences, paragraphs, and texts.

It is worth remembering that when children settle down to write, the task can be quite daunting. A good writer has to skilfully handle such basics as handwriting, spelling, and punctuation, as well as controlling sentences and thinking about what to say. Indeed, many children struggle with writing because they fall at the first post: their minds taken up by worrying over such basics as 'Where does the full stop go?'. If such basic skills are not reasonably automatic, if children are not confident at handling grammar, then their ability to compose will be held back.

This course is founded on the notion that becoming skilful at grammar actually can liberate children as writers. The more adept children are at using these skills in their writing, the more freedom they will have to focus upon the actual act of creative composition. Good writers are skilful at handling the building blocks of language. Ted Hughes knew where to put full stops; he was able to focus upon the act of creation.

Teaching sequences

Grammar Success is built around the National Literacy Framework sentence level objectives. However, where there are gaps in the framework (for instance, the omission of *nouns* from Year 3) these have been addressed. Additions and slight alterations have been made in the light of teachers' experience of using the framework in the classroom.

In planning the course, attention has been paid to ensuring that sensible links have been created between the sentence and text level objectives, and thereby to improve the ability to read and write different texts.

Each unit in *Grammar Success* facilitates the teaching of specific sentence level grammar points through a sequence of three sessions. The 'one off' lesson too often fails as children need a chance to revisit and to apply what they have been learning. To address this, each unit leads pupils through these three stages of learning, using all elements of the course:

Session 1 Introduces children to a particular sentence level feature through whole class use of OHT and consolidation in a photocopy master (PCM A).

Session 2 Investigates the use of the feature through reading and focused language work in the Pupils' Book and follow-up PCM B activity.

Session 3 Applies the feature to improve their written work, through shared and independent writing, based on work in the Pupils' Book.

Whilst a full range of texts and outcomes are provided in the Pupils' Book, children will gain greater understanding of the grammar, if they are taught all three sessions using all three elements of the course.

How the sessions work

Session 1 uses an OHT to introduce the grammatical objective to the children. This part of the session should be lively and interactive. The majority of basic grammar teaching can be accomplished through active whole-class teaching. OHTs have a number of advantages over worksheets or working on a board.

- It is easy to check that children are joining in.
- The text can be annotated in response to children's ideas. Different features can be underlined in different colours to draw attention to different aspects of a text.
- The text can be projected onto a whiteboard which can be written upon.

Once time has been spent as a whole class looking at an objective the class moves into independent activities. These are designed around a PCM that provides an activity devised to deepen children's understanding and confirm what they have been taught as a whole class. Many of the PCMs are differentiated to allow for pupils who may struggle or who need an extra challenge, or as homework.

By the end of Session 1, pupils should be in a position to define their understanding of the objective. Definition needs to relate not merely to discussing what the feature is – but also to how it is used. Pupils may like to keep a literacy glossary into which definitions and points about writing are written. Class wall charts are useful as a way of providing a reminder.

Session 2 uses the Pupils' Book, and the PCMs. The Pupils' Book activities focus upon the grammatical feature in the context of wide-ranging stimulus texts. Pupils are asked comprehension questions on each text before moving into activities that focus upon the grammatical feature in use. Session 2 thus moves children's understanding further on, by looking at the objective in context.

Movement through the session is quite simple – read the stimulus text and think about what it means. Then revisit the text and look carefully at how it has been written. In this way children are encouraged to read as writers – looking constantly at the structures and grammatical features that writers use to create texts and gain effects. The teacher's notes offer questions to ask and points to make in a whole class introduction.

This time the independent activities are in the Pupils' Book. Activity A consists of comprehension questions that dig under the skin of the text, deepening children's understanding. Activity B focuses upon the use of the sentence level feature within the text. It revisits the grammatical feature introduced in Session 1 and considers its use within a text.

The plenary, outlined in the teacher's notes, draws all the children together to reconfirm what is known about the sentence level feature. This process should put the large majority of children in the class in a position to understand the feature and to recognize how writers use it effectively within texts. References outwards to other texts are, of course, useful.

By the end, pupils have critically reflected upon the use of the objective through their reading.

Session 3 relates again to the text in the Pupils' Book, which now becomes a model for children's own writing. The teacher's notes describe in detail how to carry out shared writing, demonstrating how to use the grammatical feature in the process of drafting a new text as part of activity C.

The role of shared writing cannot be underestimated as a key approach to teaching writing. During shared writing a number of different teaching strategies can be brought into play.

1 *Demonstration* – the teacher shows children how to use the feature, talking through the writing, explaining its use as an 'expert writer'. The children's role is to sit and listen carefully. Obviously, the modelling needs to be swift and engaging or children may grow restless. However, if the teacher writes directly onto an OHT this has the advantage of being able to look at the class at a glance, aiding control and drawing children's attention to the teaching points. The teacher rehearses sentences aloud and constantly rereads, checking the writing.

2 *Whole class composition* – having demonstrated the objective in practice, the teacher moves onto involving the children in actively writing. Obviously this process has to be lively and engaging, challenging children to refine their contributions. There is a danger of merely accepting the first thought that comes into the children's heads. They should be asked to explain ideas and discuss why one idea might be more effective than another. Building in time to discuss ideas briefly in pairs is also useful as a way of involving every pupil.

3 *Supported writing* – with whiteboards or notebooks, children have an attempt at using the feature within one or two sentences. This can be supported by a list of ideas, a writing frame or by pair work. The teacher can then check that children can use the objective in a controlled situation, within a few sentences. Once confident, children can move into more extended independent composition.

A photocopiable Reminder Sheet in the Teacher's Book provides a summary, defining the grammatical feature and giving guidance on how to use it effectively in writing. This could be adapted or added to by the children in the light of their thoughts. Rudimentary understandings can be refined over time. These sheets might be added to the children's literacy glossary, put onto an OHT as a whole class reminder or enlarged and displayed as a poster.

Session 3 moves into pupils writing their own work, drawing on the shared writing experience. As pupils write independently the teacher may wish to work with a group that struggles or to stretch the top end. Children should become used to concentrating hard during writing. Just before writing, remind them of the particular features to include. Unit by unit, the pupils gain a growing repertoire of grammatical skills that they can deploy to improve their writing.

End of year hurdles

One of the difficulties that many teachers face is knowing what children should have achieved by the end of any given year. This is easy enough if you happen to be a Year 6 teacher. However, it is less clear for Year 3 teachers. The grid below provides a clear set of markers to aim for. The list relates directly to the level descriptors, the programmes of study, and the literacy framework.

Many children will achieve more than this – the grid provides a base line. A few will not reach this level.

However, the grid lists key aspects that can be used as a focus for teaching, for marking, for monitoring, and for target setting.

Of course, not everything has to be tackled at once. During the course of Year 3 children should become more adept in demonstrating the features described. If children can demonstrate these features frequently in their everyday writing, they will be on target for achieving a confident level 4.

Sentence construction	Punctuation	Language effects	Cohesion	Purpose and organization
Write simple and compound sentences. Begin to use some subordinators, e.g. *if, so, while, though, since.* Vary openings of sentences to repetition. Begin to vary sentences for different text types.	Demarcate sentences as a matter of habit in the course of writing – using full stops, capital letters, question and exclamation marks – usually accurately. Begin to use speech marks and capital letters for a range of purposes. Use commas securely in a list.	Use interesting vocabulary; vary use of adjectives and verbs for impact. Select nouns to be specific, e.g. *poodle* rather than *dog.* Use terminology appropriate to text type.	Use 1st or 3rd person and tense consistently. Use a range of connectives that signal time, e.g. *first, next, later.*	Vary story openings to create effects, such as building tension, suspense, creating moods, establishing character, and scene setting. Begin to address the reader, for instance by using questions in non-fiction. Write narratives with a *build-up,* and *complication* that leads towards a defined ending, using a paragraph for each. In non-fiction basic structure is appropriate, for instance use of introductory statement, and concluding statement. Sequence sentences to extend ideas logically. Borrow language and structures from different text types for own writing. Brainstorm words and ideas, collect suitable words and phrases before writing. Use different planning formats, e.g. *charting, mapping, flow charts, simple storyboards.* Make and use notes. Identify and consider audience and how this affects writing. Mentally revise writing, and cumulatively reread, making adaptations and corrections. Be able to improve own writing and correct errors. Use IT to polish and present.

> **End of Year 3:**
> **Statement of Objectives**

Assessing writing

Guidance on marking and assessing pupils' briefer written responses is built in to each unit in this Teacher's Book through assessment notes and model answers. This section looks at pupils' responses to the longer written tasks in activity C in the Pupil's Book. The following writing samples are by Year 3 children who have been working on Unit 15, which focuses upon agreement of verbs.

Both samples are pleasingly accurate in relation to the objective of subject/verb agreement. However, the text-level objective of the activity is to write a story opening and sample A is less successful in controlling this, at the same time as securing the sentence level objective.

If you refer to the end of year statements in the grid on page 6, the samples show that both pupils are well placed to achieve these by the end of the year. However it is clear that the pupil who wrote sample A has more progress to make than pupil B.

Sample A

Strengths in the writing

Improvements needed

Uses simple and compound sentences

Some interesting choices of vocabulary

Use of commas in a list

Begins to use broader range of connectives, showing move towards complex sentences

Strong on agreement and consistent use of tense

Sentences well demarcated and uses speech marks

Needs more detail in setting and build-up

Needs to vary sentence openings to avoid repetitiveness

Some paragraphing would help the reader

Needs to check misspellings

Some missed capital letters

Includes a rushed ending, making it too brief as a complete story and going too far for an opening

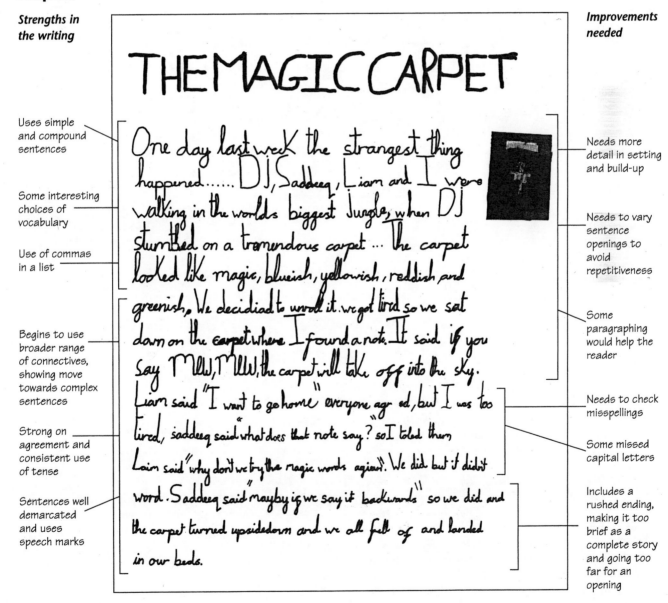

Sample B

Strengths in the writing

Improvements needed

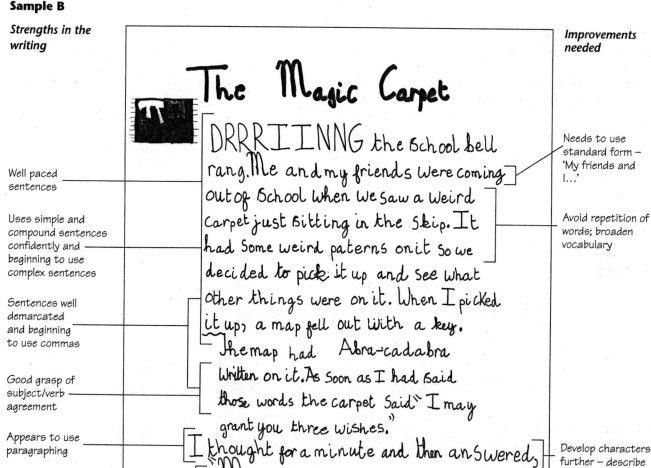

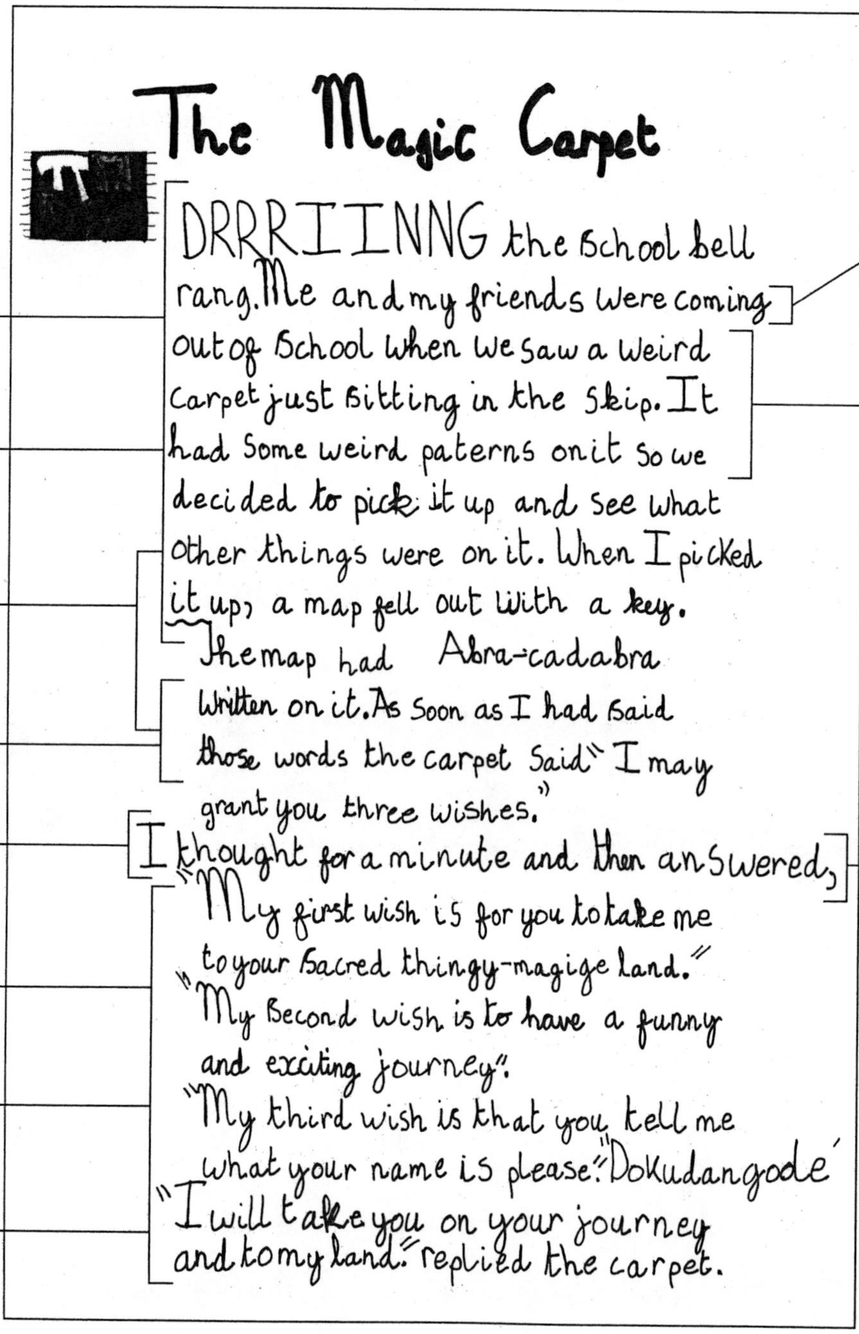

The Magic Carpet

DRRRIINNG the school bell rang. Me and my friends were coming out of school when we saw a weird carpet just sitting in the skip. It had some weird paterns on it so we decided to pick it up and see what other things were on it. When I picked it up, a map fell out with a key.

The map had Abra-cadabra written on it. As soon as I had said those words the carpet said "I may grant you three wishes."

I thought for a minute and then answered, "My first wish is for you to take me to your sacred thingy-magige land." "My second wish is to have a funny and exciting journey". "My third wish is that you tell me what your name is please." "Dokudangode" "I will take you on your journey and to my land." replied the carpet.

Strengths (left annotations):

- Well paced sentences
- Uses simple and compound sentences confidently and beginning to use complex sentences
- Sentences well demarcated and beginning to use commas
- Good grasp of subject/verb agreement
- Appears to use paragraphing
- Good use of traditional tale motif: three wishes
- Consistent use of speech marks
- Language appropriate to this type of tale

Improvements (right annotations):

- Needs to use standard form – 'My friends and I...'
- Avoid repetition of words; broaden vocabulary
- Develop characters further – describe how they think or feel

---

The principal aim of *Grammar Success* is to help children make the link between sentence level work and their reading and writing. Good writers are skilful grammarians. They become free to create, to focus upon capturing what they want to say, to manipulate the audience powerfully and purposefully. It is not for nothing that the Cornish expression says, 'The tongueless man gets his land took'. *Grammar Success* is intended to leave more children able to create, to argue their corner, to explain, to inform – so that they never 'get their land took'.

Pie Corbett

Reviewing the basics

The purpose of this unit is to secure basic sentence punctuation, and to look at using commas in simple lists. For many children, this will represent revision, with some new material relating to the use of commas.

NLS coverage

Key objective

SL 10 To identify boundaries between sentences
11 Write in complete sentences
12 To demarcate sentences with full stops and capital letters
13 To use commas to separate items in a list

Learned through:

TL Reading comprehension
19 To compare how information is presented

TL Writing composition
22 To write simple non-chronological reports, using notes made to organize and present ideas. To write for a known audience

WL 3 To practise reading and spelling high frequency words

Assessment criteria

SL By the end of this unit, pupils should be able to:
- segment continuous prose into separate sentences
- punctuate simple sentences accurately
- use sentence punctuation when reading aloud
- punctuate lists correctly

TL Writing composition
Pupils should be able to write a simple non-chronological report for a known audience

Session 1

You will need OHT 1 and PCM 1A.

Shared reading

1 Display OHT 1: *Sandwiches* (with cross-curricular links to Design Technology and Science). Explain to pupils that you will be displaying a non-fiction text – a report, which is used to classify and describe.

2 Read the text to the class, explaining that afterwards you will be discussing the main advantages and disadvantages of sandwiches. Relate this to their own experience with questions like these.
- Do you bring sandwiches? Why/why not?
- What are your favourite sandwiches?

3 Next, discuss the text: its layout and how the text is divided into paragraphs. Identify the main idea in each paragraph. Pupils may also notice that it is written in the present tense.

Sentence level work

1 Ask pupils to identify how many sentences there are in each paragraph, using these discussion points.
- Ask pupils to explain how they know the number of sentences (e.g. sentences express a complete thought, begin with a capital letter and end with a full stop). Pupils will probably cite the last two.
- Which of these indicators is the most reliable? Do all the class agree on this?
- Can they think of any other purposes for capital letters or full stops?

Children should explain their answers. They may note that capital letters are used in different ways – for proper nouns, the first word in a line of poetry – whereas full stops are only used for ending sentences. This should help them conclude that full stops are the best indicator of sentence boundaries.

2 Ask pupils if they can find any other punctuation marks in OHT 1. They should notice commas. Invite a child to come out and highlight the commas. Then guide the discussion about the use of these

commas. What do you notice about the way the commas are grouped? Do children know what the commas are being used for? Draw attention to the sentences in which the commas occur: they are lists. The commas separate the items in the list.

Look at the number of items in each list, for example sandwich fillings: *egg, cheese, tuna, ham and salad*. There are five items but only three commas: the last two items are joined by *and*.

Look at the other lists, and see if this stays true: *sugar, honey, jam, peanut butter or extra mayonnaise*. This time, the last two items are two-word phrases, joined by the word *or*.

Next, ring any commas which are not in lists. Pupils may notice that they occur with *and* and *or*. You will look at this again in the next session.

Independent activities

PCM 1A: *Tutti Fruity* offers two sentences from a report about ice-cream which have been jumbled up. Pupils will need to be guided to reconstruct the two sentences in the centre of a lined sheet, so as to allow space to write opening and closing sentences for the report.

Plenary

Encourage pupils to compare the sentences they have created using PCM 1A. Discuss and look at the model answer on page 11.

Session 2

You will need Pupils' Book Unit 1 pages 6–7 and PCM 1B.

Shared reading

1 Explain to pupils that you will be reading *Viking Settlers* in the Pupils' Book – a report about the Vikings. What do they know about the Vikings? You may wish to complete a KWL grid, or brainstorm.

2 Read the text and take the pupils' initial responses.
 ■ How much of the information in the report did you know already?
 ■ Is there any new information and is it surprising?
 ■ Are there any local place names which may be Viking in origin?

3 Next look at the structure of the report. Does it follow the same pattern as the report on *Sandwiches*? Notice that it has an introductory paragraph, and paragraphs on particular aspects of the subject. You may wish to use the Reminder Sheet from Unit 6 *Verbs in reports* that summarizes report structure.

Sentence level work

1 Review work on punctuation from previous session in the light of the *Viking Settlers* report. Look, in particular, at commas.
 ■ How many of them occur in lists?
 ■ How many are doing something else?

Their other main use in this text is to divide the sentence into two parts, as these examples show.
There are hundreds of these names in the north and east of Britain, but almost none in the south-west.
Like Anglo-Saxon place names, Viking ones often include the name of the man who first settled there.

3 Summarize by explaining that commas can separate items in a list, or separate parts of a sentence. Ask pupils to listen while you read the sentences which contain commas, where you pause fractionally. The pause in speech performs the same task as the comma in the text – it separates items in a list, etc to make it easier for listeners to understand.

Independent activities

Activity B in the Pupils' Book focuses on the two main uses of commas in the *Viking Settlers* report. Pupils identify examples and then list the use of all punctuation in the piece.

PCM 1B: *Punctuating potatoes* acts as a reinforcement to this, asking pupils to punctuate a report, identifying sentence and paragraph boundaries and then to justify their choices.

Plenary

Children feed back on their work. Which punctuation marks did they find most easy to explain in Activity B and PCM 1B? List together those which you have looked at in the past two sessions, and their purposes. Compare this list with the Reminder Sheet.

Session 3

You will need Pupils' Book Unit 1 pages 6–7 and the Reminder Sheet.

Shared writing

Look back at OHT 1: *Sandwiches* and *Viking Settlers* in the Pupils' Book. Although the topics of these texts are very different, both are reports and have a similar structure. Draw children's attention to the introductory paragraph, and the way in which each paragraph in the report covers a different aspect of the topic. Refer to the Reminder Sheet.

Write together

1 Explain that you are going to model writing a report based on a single topic of interest to the children, e.g. *Sheep*. Suggest an audience for the text, e.g. younger pupils' science lesson.

Offer an outline of the text in the report:
Paragraph 1: Introduction – setting out the topic
Paragraph 2: Appearance of sheep
Paragraph 3: Habitat of sheep
Paragraph 4: What sheep are used for
Paragraph 5: Conclusion

2 This is another opportunity to demonstrate the use of punctuation to separate sentences, and of commas in lists. Use intonation as a cue, as well as grammar. Pupils should understand that commas – like pauses in speech – serve a grammatical purpose.

Independent writing activity

This shared writing should lead directly to activity C in the Pupils' Book. Remind them of the young audience for their report and to think about how they might write the report on their local area for use as part of a web-site. Use the Reminder Sheet as needed, for support.

Plenary

Children share one paragraph from their written report. Ask classmates to listen and decide how many sentences there are in each paragraph. Confirm answers with the writer!

Assessment

Sentence level
In children's reading, refer to their use of punctuation.

When marking writing, comment upon: capital letters to start sentences; the use of full stops / question marks / exclamation marks to end sentences; and the use of commas in lists.

Writing composition
Comment on the extent to which children have grouped ideas appropriately and used paragraphs in their reports.

Model answers

Pupils' Book A

1 Denmark, Norway
2 Traded in fur and slaves, farmed, made necklaces and brooches
3 (Check place names for your area are correct.)
4 (Answers might include: *anxious, frightened, impressed.*)

Pupils' Book B

5 Items in List	Commas	Example from text
Two	none	amber necklaces and metal brooches
Three	one	slaves, fur and amber
Four	two	England, Scotland and the Isle of Man

6 *Look for commas*
7 *Britain has been invaded by many groups of people such as Romans, Vikings and Anglo Saxons. // My favourite sandwich fillings are egg, cheese, tuna and ham. // Potatoes can be cooked in many ways, for example: boiled, fried, baked, chipped.*
8 *There are hundreds of these names in the north and east of Britain, but almost none in the south-west.*
There are hundreds of these names in the north and east of Britain. There are almost none in the south-west.
9 *Capital letters – beginnings of sentences, proper nouns / names*

Full stops – ends of sentences
Commas – between items in a list, and between parts of sentences

1A   Tutti Frutti

Some pupils may create different sentences using fewer words: the main focus here is sentence construction and punctuation, so mark sentences according to this rather than whether or not all words and punctuation marks have been used. Challenge more able pupils to use all words.
There are many flavours of ice-cream, like vanilla, coconut, strawberry, chocolate or banana.
Some ice-creams have things in them.
You can buy choc chips, biscuit raisins or nuts.

1B   Punctuating Potatoes

Potatoes are a very popular food. Most people eat them every day. They are cheap and healthy to eat. // You can buy potatoes in many different forms. Some people like chips. Others like boiled, mashed, roasted or baked potatoes. Potatoes can be eaten with lots of other foods like eggs, roasts, burgers and fish. // Potatoes contain Vitamin C which makes them a healthy option, unless you put too much butter on them. They will continue to be eaten for a long time to come.

These two sentences are from a report about ice-cream. They have been jumbled up.

1 Cut up the words and rearrange them.

2 Do not forget to put the punctuation marks in.

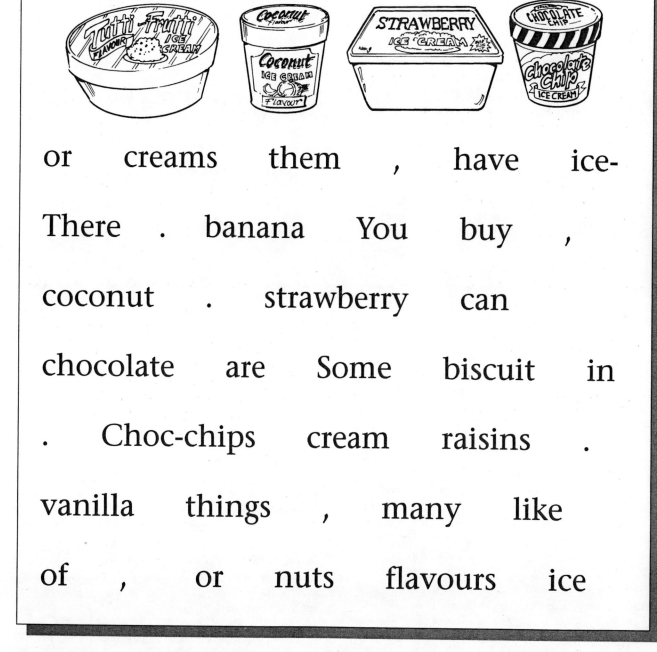

or   creams   them   ,   have   ice-

There   .   banana   You   buy   ,

coconut   .   strawberry   can

chocolate   are   Some   biscuit   in

.   Choc-chips   cream   raisins   .

vanilla   things   ,   many   like

of   ,   or   nuts   flavours   ice

3 Now write the rest of the report. You will need an opening statement about ice-cream and a final sentence. Be ready to read your report to the class and to explain how you worked it out.

Punctuating potatoes

This short report has not been punctuated at all. It is your turn to be the editor. Use a red pen or pencil to correct the punctuation.

1 Write in capital letters where they are needed.

2 Where the writer should have started a new paragraph, put in the mark //.

Potatoes are a very popular food most people eat them every day they are cheap and healthy to eat you can buy potatoes in many different forms some people like chips others like boiled mashed roasted or baked potatoes potatoes can be eaten with lots of other foods like eggs roasts burgers and fish potatoes contain vitamin c which makes them a healthy option unless you put too much butter on them they will continue to be eaten for a long time to come

3 Now complete the chart below to show why you have used the punctuation marks. Use the back of the sheet if you need more space.

Punctuation mark	Number	Reason why
Full stops Commas Capital letters New paragraph Other punctuation marks		

Sentence punctuation

As well as words, we use the tone of our voices, small pauses and gestures to help people understand what we are saying and how we feel about it.

When we write we cannot do this, so we use punctuation marks to help readers understand.

- Capital letters (e.g. H, B, G) tell us where sentences start, and tell us when words are names.
- Full stops (.) tell readers where sentences end.
- Commas (,) tell readers how to separate sentences into parts which make sense. They can be used to separate items in a list or to separate two parts of a sentence.

Punctuation helps readers to understand what we write, and also helps them when they are reading aloud.

When you have a piece of writing, ask a friend to read what you have written aloud to you. If they cannot make sense of it, that might be because of the punctuation. Look at it together and see if you can work out a better way to punctuate it.

Report writing

1 A report is one type of information text. A report is useful because it gives the readers information on a particular subject.

2 A report:
- Begins with an introduction telling us one of the most important facts about the subject.
- Then gives us more information about the subject in separate paragraphs.
- Finishes with an interesting fact about the subject.

Speech punctuation

The purpose of this unit is to teach children to identify dialogue in texts, to read it with expression; children will look at how writers use dialogue in stories and punctuate it accurately.

NLS coverage

Key objective

SL 2 To take account of basic conventions of speech punctuation when reading aloud
7 To identify speech marks in reading, to begin to use in own writing, and to use capital letters to mark the start of direct speech
8 Use the term *speech marks*

Learned through:

TL **Reading comprehension**
2 How dialogue is presented in stories; use paragraphing to organize dialogue
3 To be aware of the different voices in stories, showing differences between the narrator and different characters used

TL **Writing composition**
10 Using reading as a model, to write own passages of dialogue
15 To begin to use paragraphing in presentation of dialogue in stories

WL 17 To generate synonyms for high frequency words, e.g. *said*
18 To use the term 'synonym'
19 To generate common vocabulary for introducing and concluding dialogue, e.g. *said, replied, asked*; collect examples from reading

Assessment criteria

SL By the end of this unit pupils should be able to:
- identify dialogue in stories
- explain the conventions for punctuating dialogue: speech marks, use of capital letters at the beginning of direct speech
- notice some other aspects of speech punctuation, e.g. use of commas, punctuation within direct speech, etc.
- use speech marks when writing dialogue

TL **Writing composition**
Pupils should be able to write a passage of dialogue

Session 1

You will need OHT 2 and PCM 2A.

Shared reading

OHT 2: *Walking Home* is a short piece of narrative including dialogue. There are three characters – two children and their mother. Before displaying and reading it, ask the pupils to discuss occasions when they have arrived home late. Display and read OHT 2.

1 Read the text and take initial reactions from the class.

- Where do pupils think Michelle and Andrew may have been? Are there any clues in the text?
- Which character is more anxious? What evidence is there for this in the text?
- How does the mother feel when they arrive home? Which child is right about her reaction?

2 Seek three volunteers to read the parts of the characters, and one to be the narrator. Ask these pupils to reread the text with expression and get other class members to comment on their use of expression.

3 Ask children why the writer uses dialogue. Does it tell us anything about the setting, the characters, or the plot? Children should use examples from the text to support their arguments.

Sentence level work

1 Explain that you are going to look at the way speech is punctuated. Initially, discuss why speech is punctuated.
   ■ Would it be easy to read stories with dialogue if there were no speech marks?

2 Ask pupils to look at the different sorts of punctuation marks used in the dialogue.
   They should focus on: speech marks and capital letters. Make sure that pupils understand that the speech occurs only within speech marks. Practising the reading of dialogue without the intervening narrative will reinforce this point.

3 Comment upon the verbs used by the writer. Identify them as verbs and ask children to read lines from the dialogue with appropriate expression. Build up a bank of verbs together, which writers use and which pupils could use in their own writing.

Independent activities

Use PCM 2A: *Improving the speech*. This offers children a chance to punctuate direct speech in text, to identify, and to change speech verbs. They should be encouraged to tackle the basic punctuation task first and then the task of improving the speech verbs to give more clues to the reader as to expression.

Plenary

Invite individual children to select one sentence that they have rewritten from *Improving the speech* to show their choice of speech verb. Ask them to read the sentence aloud to the class and invite feedback.

Session 2

You will need Pupils' Book Unit 2 pages 8–9 and PCM 2B.

Shared reading

Before turning to *The Whales' Song* from the Pupils' Book, remind the class about the way in which dialogue can be used to tell readers more about characters and their feelings.

1 Explain that you will be reading another text which involves three characters, this time a child, her uncle, and her grandmother.

2 Tell the children that during shared reading, they should think about the characters involved and what we can learn from what they say and how they say it. Then read *The Whales' Song* to the children.

3 Organize pupils into pairs and ask them each to talk about the text and write down one adjective for: Lilly, her grandmother, and her uncle. Allow five minutes for the discussion.
   Children should look for evidence from the text. If they find this difficult, draw their attention to:
   ■ Words the characters actually use
   ■ Words the writer uses to describe their speech or their movement
   ■ Punctuation – for example, Uncle Frederick has a lot of exclamation marks!
   Collate the adjectives pupils have come up with. Is there any agreement in their choices?

4 Drawing on the discussion, list the strategies the writer uses to convey each character.

Sentence level work

1 Reread the text with the children.
   ■ What do they notice about the speech marks here? They may have already noticed that there is only one mark, not two as is more conventional. Ask children why they think this is?
   ■ Who chose this – was it a mistake? Did the writer choose, the editor or publisher?
   ■ Does it make any difference that it is one or two speech marks?

2 Look at the other conventions, for example that each new utterance begins with a capital letter. Do these still hold true for this text?

3 Formulate some hypotheses about why this convention has been used. Maybe it is because the text was written by writers from other countries, or maybe it is to do with the publisher.

4 Discuss how the children could investigate this by looking at the conventions chosen in other narratives including dialogue. This activity should demonstrate that use of two inverted commas is more common than one. Suggest to pupils that they conform to this convention.

Independent activities

Both the Pupils' Book activities and PCM 2B: *Collecting Verbs* encourage children to focus on verbs used in dialogue.
   PCM 2B offers more structure for collecting and using speech verbs for less able pupils.

Plenary

Ask pupils to practise reading dialogue from *The Whales' Song* in role. Their aim is to create a convincing dramatized reading.

Session 3

You will need OHT 2, Pupils' Book Unit 2 pages 8–9, and the Reminder Sheet.

Shared writing

Begin by reviewing OHT 2: *Walking Home* and revising the purposes of dialogue. Writers put it in for reasons: to tell readers more about the characters, and to give them clues about the setting and about what's happening in the story.

Explain that you are going to write a short passage of dialogue, based on another conversation between Michelle, Andrew, and their mother. The children are trying to persuade their mother that they should be allowed to go to a fair. She will eventually allow them to go with her or an older cousin/family friend. Discuss the moods of the characters, the plot and introduce the Reminder Sheet.

Writing together

1 Begin by writing a few lines of the dialogue.

'Mum, can we go to the fair at Dingley Field on Saturday?' asked Andrew.

'Hm, I'm not sure. It could be really crowded,' replied Mum.

'Oh, please, Mum,' moaned Michelle, 'all our friends are going…'

2 Demonstrate speech punctuation as you are writing, using all features of speech punctuation, but focusing strongly on speech marks and paragraphing.

3 Remind children that the characters need to come through the speech.

Independent writing activity

This shared session above should lead straight into activity C in the Pupils' Book. Distribute the Reminder Sheet for support as needed.

Plenary

Pupils present a dramatized reading of their dialogue based on *The Whales' Song*. Other class members can then comment on the extent to which the dialogue reveals more about the characters and what is happening in the story.

Assessment

Sentence level
In guided reading, ask children to identify passages of dialogue and to identify punctuation linked with dialogue.
In writing, children should be able to use speech marks. Comment on more advanced punctuation where children have used it.

Writing composition
Children will produce a punctuated passage of dialogue. Comment on its function in the text; what does it reveal about the characters?

Model answers

Pupils' Book ⬜ A

1 *Lilly's grandmother loved the whales. She brought them gifts*

2 *Singing*

3 *She is in a happy mood, she is remembering happy things*

4 *Meat, bones and blubber*

5 *He's in a bad mood. He stomps and snaps and grumbles, and he says rude things like calling Lilly's grandmother an 'old fool'.*

Pupils' Book ⬜ B

6 Lilly: *asked*
Grandmother: *smiled, sighed, whispered, continued*
Uncle Frederick: *snapped, grumbled*

⬜ 2A   Improving the speech 🔊

Only speech punctuation is included here. Do not be concerned if pupils have not used commas to separate speech from narration. However, they should have control over speech marks, and use of capitals. Pupils may have used a range of alternatives to *said*.

"Let's go and see the lions first!"

"Oh no," said Charlotte, "I want to see the seals!"

"Come on," she said, "let's do something we can all enjoy. What about the monkeys?"

"Look at that one over there," said James. "He's scratching himself!"

"There are some babies over there!" said Susan.

Susan said "Good ideas. What about you, James?"

Here is a part of a story which has some speech in it. The editor has returned it because there are some problems.

■ The writer has forgotten to punctuate the speech properly.

■ The writer has used the word *said* too often.

1 Read the text and put in speech marks and capital letters with a red pencil.

2 Look at each *said* and write in a better verb to replace it.

Crying at the Zoo

Susan took Charlotte and James to the zoo for the day. It was a long way, and they had to get up very early. There were lots of things to do when they got there.

"Let's go and see the lions first!   said James.

"oh no "   said Charlotte,   I want to see the seals "

Poor Susan! Charlotte and James both started crying.

Come on,   she said, "let's do something we can all enjoy. What about the monkeys?"

They all went over to see the monkeys.

"Look at that one over there,   said James. "He's scratching himself!"

"There are some babies over there!" said Susan.

Charlotte said that she would like some chips. Susan said, "good idea. What about you James?

James didn't say anything. He had fallen asleep!

Look through your reading books.

1 Collect verbs writers use for speech. Decide what they tell you about how the character is feeling and write them into the table below. Two have been done for you!

Happy	Sad
cheered	moaned
....	....
....	....
....	....
....	....

Scared	Other feelings
....	....
....	....
....	....
....	....

2 Use verbs from your table to complete the sentences below. Remember that the verbs tell you about how the speaker is feeling.

"Look, Mum, a circus!" .... Sarah.

"I don't want to go to bed yet," .... Matthew.

"It's raining again," .... Rahim.

"Can I have some more cake, Dad?" .... Ben.

2 *Speech punctuation*

Reasons for speech in stories

Writers use speech in stories for three main reasons.

- To help readers learn more about the characters who are talking.
- To tell readers more about what is happening in the story.
- To stop readers from getting bored.

Punctuating speech

In stories, speech has special sorts of punctuation.

- The words the person actually says are put inside speech marks: " at the beginning and " at the end.
- Each time a different person starts talking the speech goes on a new line.
- Each time a new person starts talking, the first word they say starts with a capital letter.

Text presentation

The purpose of this unit is to allow children to investigate a range of alternative ways of presenting text, focusing on writers' and editors' reasons for choosing to present text in these ways.

NLS coverage

Key objective

SL 9 Notice and investigate a range of other devices for presenting texts, e.g. enlarged or italicized print, captions and headings, inset text; explore purposes and collect examples

Learned through:

TL Reading comprehension
20 To read passages of non-fiction, and identify the main points of the text

TL Writing composition
21 To make a simple record of information from texts, drawing together notes from more than one source

WL 13 Collect new words from reading and work in other subjects and create ways of categorizing and logging them
14 Infer the meaning of unknown words from context

Assessment criteria

SL By the end of this unit, pupils should be able to:
- recognize and name a range of devices for presenting texts
- explain reasons for use of these devices
- begin to use these devices in their own writing

TL Writing composition
Pupils should be able to make notes on a topic of interest, drawing from more than one source

Session 1

You will need OHT 3, a slip of paper or a whiteboard per pair of pupils and PCM 3A.

Shared reading

1 Explain to pupils that you are going to read a passage of information about materials. Ask them what they already know about materials, and record their ideas on a topic web.

2 Ask pupils to work in pairs give each pair a slip of paper or a whiteboard. Get them to decide upon and write down one question about materials that they would like answered.

3 Display OHT 3: *Materials* and read it through with the class taking their initial responses. Then talk around these questions.

- Have you found the answer to the question you wrote down before reading the text?
- Has anyone not found the answer to their question?
- Where could these answers be found?

4 Reread the text. Identify and underline the main pieces of information in the text. Discuss what a reader might do with this information – leave it marked in the text so, that when you return to it, it is clear or make notes.

5 Discuss the structure of each section of the text. Look closely at the first section. It covers:
- Origin of material
- Description
- Usage

Sentence level work

1 Look at the ways information is presented in this text. Ask pupils how many different font variations

there are. They should notice that as well as the basic type there is a larger text, italicized, and emboldened text. Investigate why these have been used, i.e.:

- Larger type for headings
- Italics for adjectives which describe the material
- Bold for three different groups nouns – the original source of materials; varieties of the materials; items which may be made from the material

2 Consider the impact of using different fonts.
- Does it make the text easier – or more difficult – to read?
- Does it make it easier to extract information from the text?

Underline the fact that its purpose is to draw attention to the information, so that readers can access it more easily. Can pupils think of other ways of drawing attention to specific items? They may suggest – use of colour, inset text boxes, underlining, or use of a completely different font.

Independent activities

Ask pupils to collect non-fiction texts, to select three to examine in detail. Their task is to look at alternative ways in which text is presented and to record these text features, using PCM 3A: *Comparing texts*.

Plenary

Invite pupils to feed back on what they have discovered. Discuss how many different types of text have been found in any one text. Consider whether and how too many text features can be confusing or distracting.

Session 2

You will need Pupils' Book Unit 3 pages 10–11 and PCM 3B.

Shared reading

1 Before turning to *Staying on the Road* in the Pupils' Book, ask children if they know how cars stay on the road. What parts of the car are involved? Model completion of a chart (see PCM 3B: *Gathering information*) to gather known information and predictions. Encourage pupils to use a grid like this when reading about other subjects.

2 Read *Staying on the Road* with pupils. Review the chart with them. Which guesses were correct? Check for additional information. Discuss how

children could find out more about the topic and list these possibilities.

Sentence level work

1 Focus on the different ways in which text has been presented in *Staying on the Road*. Look at the different parts of the text. The main body of the text covers general points about suspension. There is also a diagram of a wheel with captions that each explain the function of a part of the suspension mechanism.
- Has the use of emboldened text, inset boxes in different colours and captions helped to get the information across clearly?
- What is the main purpose of these captions?

2 Discuss text clues that might show links to other parts of the text. For example, the use of bold for difficult key words. You can reveal that this is a signal to readers that these words were included in a glossary.

Independent activities

As a reinforcement, activity A asks pupils to summarize key information from *Staying on the Road*. For activity B they will need two single-page information texts with some contrasting features at an appropriate reading level.

Plenary

Discuss guidelines for presenting texts in different ways. Start by asking how many different text presentation features are helpful on one page? Can writers use too many?

Session 3

You will need Pupils' Book Unit 3 pages 10–11, OHT 3, and the Reminder Sheet.

Shared writing

1 Explain to children that you will be writing about the materials that are used to make cars. Select an appropriate audience. Would children in Year 2 be interested? Would parents be interested? Explain that as you are writing you will need to think about vocabulary which might be new to your audience, and which vital information may need to be emphasized.

2 Explore possibilities for laying out the text. Refer back to the shared texts: one contains information

about cars, the other about materials. How can these be drawn together?

Suggest including a diagram of a car, with extended captions. Discuss the advantages of diagrams over pure text, i.e. they help readers visualize, and make sense of the text.

Plan the layout of the page with these elements: a heading, introductory paragraph, a central diagram (not too large – consider how much space is needed for writing), with space for captions.

Write together

1 Compose a title, and the introductory paragraph. Make sure that pupils understand that the purpose of this paragraph is to simply explain the content of the text.

Decide how many captions you are going to write – three or four will be plenty.

2 Now consider the content – which materials are used in cars? Refer back to OHT 3: *Materials*. Can its paragraph structure be adapted for these captions? Use one paragraph to demonstrate writing of a caption, taking this approach:
  ■ Source
  ■ Where it is used in the car
  ■ Description of properties that are used in the car

This puts the information in a slightly different order, so that it links the properties of the material directly to their use in the car, and could therefore be an explanation.

Take one paragraph and model its transformation into a caption for the diagram. Model the use of different text presentation devices as you write.

Independent writing activity

This shared writing should lead pupils to activity C. They are asked to select one or two captions to write up. They may need a photocopy of OHT 3 as a source. Select some pairs to write onto OHTs, so that their work can be shared with the rest of the class and adapted. Remind these pupils to space their work well to allow for revision and editing.

Plenary

Identify another material from OHT 3 and ask which pupils have written it up as a caption. Compare versions. Discuss with the class and draw up a final version. Review any captions that have been written by pairs on OHTs.

Assessment

Sentence level
In writing, comment on the extent to which children have used a range of devices. Make sure that they do not use too many. Discuss with them their reasons for selecting specific devices.

Writing composition
Comment on the extent to which children have in their notes:
• chosen appropriate sources
• identified key ideas
• summarized in a way which can be read later

Model answers

Pupils' Book ◁ A

1 *Tyres, springs and dampers*

2

Car part	What it does	What would happen if it wasn't there?
tyres	absorb bumps/ grip road	car would slip over road surface
springs	absorb bumps	car would jump over bumps
dampers	control springiness of springs	tyres would bounce on road after bumps

Pupils' Book ◁ B

3 Answers will include references to: bold, italic, different type, and underlined type being used to draw attention to specific parts of the text; headings and sub-headings for organization and sub-division of text for clarity; captions to give details about illustrations and more information on the topic in question.

Choose three non-fiction books. Look through each one, and see which different text features it has. Put a tick or cross against them in the table below. When you complete each one, write a comment about how interesting the text looks. This activity sheet *3A* has been done for you.

Type	Activity sheet	Text A	Text B	Text C
Title	Comparing texts			
Underlined	✗			
Bold	✔			
Italic	✔			
Heading	✔			
Sub-heading	✗			
Caption	✗			
Other	✗			
Comment	The table is clear and easy to use.			

3B *Gathering information*

Complete this chart to show what you know about the topic and what you predict about it.

Topic: Was I right?	Source: Now I would like to know
I think that	
I think that	
I think that	
I think that	

Writing captions

1 Remember that each caption for the diagram will have the same structure. You should write about:

- where the material comes from, or how it is made
- where the material is used in the car. Remember there may be more than one use for some materials. Think of the main ones
- what the material is like, and explain why it is used in cars

2 As you are writing, think about the readers. You may want to make some parts of the text stand out, for example:

- words they may not have read before
- important information

There are a number of different ways of doing this. You could use bold print, italics, underlining, or capitals. You could also write some words in larger letters.

Using verbs

The purpose of this unit is to introduce children to verbs, their use in sentences and their creative use in poetry.

NLS coverage

Key objective

SL 3 To understand the function of verbs in sentences through: noticing that sentences cannot make sense without them; collecting and classifying examples of verbs from reading and own knowledge; experimenting with changing simple verbs in sentences and discussing the impact on meaning
5 To use the term *verb* appropriately

Learned through:

TL Reading comprehension
6 To read aloud and recite poems; to discuss choice of words and phrases that describe and create impact, e.g. adjectives, powerful and expressive verbs, e.g. *stare* instead of *look*
7 To express their views about a story or a poem, identifying specific words and phrases to support their viewpoint

TL Writing composition
12 To write poems using repetitive phrases and imaginative comparisons

WL 17 To generate synonyms for high-frequency words

Assessment criteria

SL By the end of this unit, pupils should be able to:
- simply explain the job of a verb in a sentence
- spot a verb in a sentence
- spot when a sentence does not have a verb
- spot when a sentence might be improved by changing and *strengthening* a verb
- use the term *verb* in discussion

WC Pupils should be able to write poems with simple patterns and repetitive phrases

Session 1

You will need OHT 4A and PCM 4A.

Shared reading

1 Explain that you will be looking at what a verb is, how sentences need them, and how a well-chosen verb can make sentences more powerful. Display OHT 4A: *The Terrible Tribe*.

2 Cover the bottom half of the OHT so that the first six lines of the poem are showing. Read these through with the class and take initial reactions.
- What do you notice at first?
- Which is your favourite name?
- Which line creates the best picture?
- Which words do you like best?

- If you could buy a word to use in their writing, which one would you use?

3 Now look more closely at the pattern. Give pupils several moments to discuss, in pairs, the basic pattern. Points that might need teasing out:
- Each sentence starts with the cat's name
- It always says 'Bill, the (adjective) cat...'
- The cat's name and the adjective always start with the same letter
- The adjective helps to suggest what the cat will be doing

Use different coloured pens to show the pattern, underlining: first names, adjectives, the word *cat*, the verb.

Sentence level work

1 Explain that in this poem the verbs tell the reader what the cat is doing and that verbs are the words

or phrases that show what is happening in a sentence. Use the term *verb* and expect the children to use it as well. Of course, some children will already know what a verb is. Let them select the verb that they think is most effective and explain why.

2 Now reveal the second half of the poem. Read it through with the class and prompt an initial discussion.
   ■ Why don't the sentences make sense – what is missing?
   ■ What does this tell them about verbs? – a good place to make the point that a verb is like the engine of the sentence. Without the engine, the sentence won't work.

3 Reread each sentence and take suggestions for each verb. Encourage the children to look for clues – in the adjectives and in the second half of the sentence. Ask them to read the whole sentence dropping their suggested verb in.

4 To summarize this opening session you could write several simple sentences on a board.
   The dog ran down the road.
   The parrot flew through the air.
   The policeman shouted at the thief.

   Decide together which word in the sentence is the verb. Ask:
   ■ Which word tells you what is happening?
   ■ Which word tells you what the dog/parrot/ policeman is doing?

   Underline in a strong colour so the children can see where the verb lies in the sentence. Iterate that the verb is the engine of the sentence. Try reading the sentence without the verb. Can the class hear how, without the engine, the sentence will not work?

Independent activities

Use PCM 4A: *Spot the verbs*. Read the poem through with the class. Discuss with them what do they like/dislike/notice about the poem? The pupils' task is to underline the verb or verbs in each sentence. You may wish to do the first with the class.

Ask them to decide which they think are the three most effective verbs. Target a weaker group for extra support, if need be. All pupils should attempt this activity. Those who finish early could illustrate each verse and then add extra verses.

Plenary

1 Reread the poem with pupils identifying verbs. Get them to say which are the verbs.

2 Take out some verbs and discuss alternatives, e.g. I *pat* the soft fur could become *tap, stroke, touch,*

blow on, caress, feel, poke, nudge, etc.

3 Make a wall chart stating that: *A verb is a word in a sentence that tells you what is happening or being done.* List a few suggested examples.

Session 2

You will need Pupils' Book Unit 4 pages 12–13 and PCM 4B.

Shared reading

1 Use *Greedy Dog* from the Pupils' Book. Read the poem through several times and discuss initial reactions. Pupils' likes, dislikes, puzzles, and patterns can be identified and shared.

2 Ask them to list three things that the dog should definitely not be eating.

3 Then get them to list three things that it might be sensible for it to eat.

Sentence level work

Read through and identify verbs. List other verbs that might be used to describe a dog. To do this write *The dog...* on a board. Then begin to take suggestions for what the dog might do:
e.g. *The dog runs, the dog leaps, the dog bounds*

Just before the children begin their independent work, reread the poem together, with plenty of expression.

Independent activities

Direct the pupils to activities in A and B in the Pupils' Book.

Early finishers and more able should use PCM 4B: *Swap the verbs*. On this sheet the verbs have been swapped round in each paragraph.

Plenary

Children feedback on their answers to activities in A and B. Make a class list of synonyms for *eat*. You may wish to set preparation of a reading of the poem for homework. Pupils can rehearse their reading in groups and should be encouraged to think about:
■ How soft or loud the lines should be
■ Who should read which lines
■ Reading with expression loudly enough to be heard
■ How fast or slow the lines should be read

Session 3

You will need Pupils' Book Unit 4 pages 12–13 and the Reminder Sheet

Shared writing

Reread PCM 4B or, if this has been used as homework, a group might perform the poem aloud. Explain that the class is going to write a simple cat poem based on *Greedy Dog* but titled *Lively Cat*. In this, pupils will be trying to use powerful verbs.

Write together

1 Begin the poem by writing up the opening line:
This cat will do anything.

   She...

2 Ask pupils to think about different things that cats do and list these things up on a board.
   e.g. *sleep, doze, purr, creep, weave, wander, run, leap, bound, drink, eat, sip, lick, nuzzle, jump, dodge, climb.*

3 Show them how to take a verb and add to the idea:
This cat will do anything.

   She sleeps in a ball all day.
   She dozes at the foot of my bed.
   She purrs when I tickle her chin...

Independent writing activity

The shared writing should lead straight into pupils attempting their own list poem, based on the same pattern.

Plenary

Create a reminder sheet with the children, using these prompts, or use the one provided on page 32 to identify key points.

■ What is a verb? (It's the word which tells you what is happening/the engine of the sentence.)
■ What job does it do in a sentence? (Gives it action/moves sentence along/tells the reader what is happening.)
■ What happens to sentences without a verb? (They don't work/don't make sense/they die.)
■ How can we use verbs to make our writing effective? (Choose powerful verbs that tell the reader exactly how something is being done. For instance, use *stare* instead of *look*.)

Assessment

Sentence level
Pupils should be able to identify obvious verbs within sentences. Ensure that they do not write sentences without verbs (though this is unlikely).

Writing composition
Pupils should be able to write a simple poem using a repetitive line. They should be used to locate verbs which might be changed to provide more impact. When marking, underline any weak use of verbs for pupils to improve.

Model answers

Pupils' Book A

1 *Greedy*
2 Answers might include: *Milk you poured out for the cat, hide your chocolates, even eat your handkerchief, conceal your socks, leave some soup without a lid.*
3 *By taking your socks or stealing soup*
4 *He does not like them, they taste peculiar, etc.*
5 *He thinks the dog is a scoundrel – but quite a character, he is fond of the dog and irritated at the same time, etc.*

Pupils' Book B

6 Powerful verbs – *poured, ties, relishes, hide, conceal, gobbling*
   Verbs instead of eat – *gobble, munch, crunch, nibble, scoff, wolf, consume, chomp, champ, bolt, chew, gnaw, graze, gorge, gulp, guzzle, slurp, feast, etc.*
7 e.g. *This dog will guzzle anything.*
   He'll even scoff your handkerchief.

4A a Spot the verbs
Verbs are – *pat, tickle, rolls, stroke, listen, purr, tug, nudge, blow, sneezes*

4B Swap the verbs
Sugar sleeps *at the end of my bed. He* wakes *up early every morning. He* stretches *himself and then* cleans *his fur with his pink tongue. He* purrs *if I stroke him.*

Sugar jumps *down and runs downstairs. He* sips *his milk and* eats *the cat food. He* pushes *his way through the cat flap and* goes *out.*

Cars rush *down our street. Sugar* stops *at the edge of the road. He* looks *first one way and then the other. He* waits *till no cars are coming and then he* trots *safely across.*

He sneaks *into the shop over the road. He* jumps *onto the counter when no-one is looking. One day he* stole *a piece of bacon. Mrs Gradshaw* chased *Sugar down the street. He* ran *too quickly for her.*

Read the poem and underline the verb or verbs in each sentence.

Touching My Cat, Sugar

I pat
the soft fur
along his
thin back.

I tickle
his black tummy
till he rolls over.

I stroke
his fur
and listen to
him
purr
like a soft engine.

I tug
gently on his tail.
And nudge
him
with my bare toes.

I blow gently
on his nose
till he sneezes.

The verbs in each of these paragraphs have been swapped around.
Write the right verb in the right sentence to make each make sense.

Sugar stroke at the end of my bed. He
stretches up early every morning. He purrs
himself and then wakes his fur with his
pink tongue. He cleans if I sleeps him.

Sugar sips down and goes downstairs. He
jumps his milk and runs the cat food. He eats
his way through the cat flap and pushes out.

Cars stops down our street. Sugar trots at
the edge of the road. He waits first one way
and then the other. He rush till no cars are
coming and then he looks safely across.

He looking into the shop over the road.
He stole onto the counter when no-one is
ran. One day he jumps a piece of bacon.
Mrs Gradshaw sneaks Sugar down the street.
He chased too quickly for her.

What is a verb?

A verb is the word or phrase which shows what is happening in a sentence.

■ Sentences need verbs or they do not make sense.

■ A verb is like the engine of a sentence. If you leave out the engine, the sentence will not work.

> This sentence does not make sense.
>
> *The red lorry the bridge.*
>
> It needs a verb.
>
> *The red lorry crossed the bridge.*

Choosing verbs

■ Choose verbs carefully. You can often find a powerful verb to tell the reader exactly how something is happening.

> The verb in this sentence is weak, it does not tell the reader *how* the burglar looked in at the window.
>
> *The burglar looked in the window.*
>
> It would be more effective with a more powerful verb than *looked*.
>
> *The burglar peered in the window.*

5 *Story verbs*

The purpose of this unit is to help children to become consistent in their use of past or present tenses when writing stories and to use powerful and expressive verbs when writing.

NLS coverage

Key objective

SL 3 To understand the function of verbs in sentences through: collecting and classifying examples of verbs from reading and own knowledge; experimenting with changing simple verbs in sentences and discussing the impact on meaning
4 To use verb tenses with increasing accuracy in writing; use past tense consistently for narration
5 To use the term *verb* appropriately

Learned through:

TL **Reading comprehension**
2 How dialogue is presented in stories
3 To be aware of different voices in stories
8 To express their views about a story, identifying specific words and phrases to support their viewpoint

TL **Writing composition**
10 Using reading as a model to write own passages of dialogue

WL 19 common vocabulary for introducing and concluding dialogue, e.g. *said, replied, asked*; collect examples from reading

Assessment criteria

SL By the end of this unit, pupils should be able to:
■ identify verbs
■ have begun to build a collection of interesting verbs
■ experiment with creating stronger meaning by changing verbs in sentences
■ use the term *verb* when talking about reading and writing
■ use tenses consistently when writing
■ spot when tenses are not used consistently when reading, and rereading

TL **Writing composition**
Pupils should be able to write a passage of dialogue, choosing interesting speech verbs.

Session 1

You will need OHT 5 and PCM 5A.

Shared reading

1 Explain that you will be looking at how verbs can be used to make story writing powerful, especially in dialogue. Throughout this session, remember to encourage children to use the term *verb*. Display OHT 5: *George Speaks*.

2 Introduce the extract from *George Speaks* by Dick King-Smith. Explain that Laura, who is seven, has been asked to look after her new baby brother,

George, who is asleep in his carry-cot. Read the OHT extract through with the class and take their initial responses, especially to Laura and George.
■ What does Laura think about the baby at the start of the extract?
■ Why might she think/feel like that?
■ Which words tell you that she is surprised?
■ How does George speak to Laura?
■ Why do you think she 'whispered'?
■ What might happen next?

3 Having listened to the children's ideas about the two characters, ask them to work in pairs and reread the passage deciding how each character might speak. As a class, listen to several examples and discuss the level, tone and expression of each.

Sentence level work

1 Use a coloured marker to identify the more obvious verbs in the passage, such as:
wake, said, tell, look, opened, stared, gasped, ran, tingled, whispered, say, make, talk, run, turned, dash, creased, understand, etc.

2 Discuss whether some of the *'said's* could be replaced by a more descriptive speech verb, such as: muttered, mumbled, hissed, etc. Brainstorm a possible list of these and then discuss why some choices might be more appropriate, i.e. as they fit with the meaning of the passage.

3 Ask pupils to reread the altered pieces of dialogue, changing the expression in light of the chosen speech verb.

4 Next focus on the verb tense of the extract. Ask when the story happened – present or past? Emphasize the difference by transforming several lines into the present tense. Remind pupils that most stories take place in the past tense.

5 Summarize this opening session by pointing out that:
   ■ A well-chosen speech verb can tell the reader how a character speaks, thinks and feels
   ■ Many narrative stories are in the past tense

Independent activities

Using PCM 5A: *Matching the feelings.* Read the passage through with the class. The task is to transform the speech verbs, so that they reflect how the characters think and feel as they speak. Start by tackling several verbs as a class. Emphasize that decisions have to be made on the basis of the context.
■ Does Jake scream, yell or hiss with fear his words?

Then get pupils to work in pairs to reread the passage and decide on the most effective speech verb to replace *said.* They should read aloud their versions, using expression to reflect their chosen speech verb. Prepare them for sharing these in the plenary and for justifying their choices.

   Some children may opt for the word *said* plus an adverb (*she said calmly*). Sometimes this works well, but you may be able to suggest that they replace this combination with one well-chosen speech verb. For instance, *she said quietly*, might be stronger *she whispered.*

Plenary

Return to PCM 5A. Listen to pupils' versions with speech verbs and discuss how successful telling the reader how a character feels or

Session 2

You will need Pupils' Book Unit 5 pages 14–15 and PCM 5B.

Shared reading

1 As a class, read through *A Gift from Winklesea* from the Pupils' Book several times – at first to get the gist of the extract and then with more expression.

2 Initial discussion with pupils could focus upon:
   ■ What leads up to these events?
   ■ What might happen next?

3 Encourage pupils to practise different ways of speaking for the family members, as they read the text again.

Sentence level work

1 Ask who can remember what a verb is. Seek examples in the extract, especially speech verbs.

2 Distinguish between the past and present by turning some verbs into present so that *said* becomes *says.* Recap that most stories are written as if they happened a while ago, and so the verbs are in the past tense.

Independent activities

1 Activities A and B in the Pupils' Book focus upon the following:
   ■ Collecting speech verbs and powerful verbs. (A summarizing class wall list could be useful to assist in selecting verbs during shared writing.)
   ■ Transforming verbs – improving sentences by selecting powerful verbs. Pupils are asked to improve five sentences from the passage where another verb might have been more effective. They should be prepared to report back, explaining how their changes add to the meaning.

2 PCM 5B: *Which verb tense?* could be used by early finishers or as a guided session. On this sheet there are three extracts from different stories. The task is to decide whether these were written in the present or past tense. A simple way into this is to ask pupils to decide which of the stories happened in the past and which are written as if they are happening now. They should decide when the story took place (past/present) and list which words suggest this.

   Pupils can then move on to transform one or more of the extracts into a different tense. You may need to demonstrate how to do this, either to the whole class or from group to group.

Plenary

During this time, check the following:

■ Examples of speech verbs instead of *said* – to be summarized into a wall chart for pupils to use when writing

■ Examples of verbs in past tense – re-emphasize the difference between past and present. (Remind pupils how *recounts* are in the past tense because they are about what has happened.)

■ Improvements made to sentences from the Pupils' Book extract

■ Ideas of verbs to use instead of *went* and *looked*

Session 3

You will need Pupils' Book Unit 5 pages 14–15, or PCM 5B and the Reminder Sheet.

Shared writing

Use the Reminder Sheet to emphasize points already made. Reread the extract from the Pupils' Book. Refer the class to collections they have made of speech verbs, or synonyms for common verbs such as *went*.

Write together

Use shared writing to continue the story in the Pupils' Book extract. You will only need to write a short amount.

Pause at verbs and discuss possible alternatives. Use the growing word list of speech/powerful verbs. Read aloud what is said and challenge the children to suggest an appropriate speech verb. Experiment with a weak verb and see if pupils suggest something stronger. Emphasize and reinforce how speech is laid out,

referring to Reminder Sheet for Speech punctuation (Unit 2 page 20) that shows how to set out dialogue.

Independent writing activity

Following directly on from shared writing, pupils should continue the extract from the Pupils' Book. Alternatively they can use one of the extracts from PCM 5B. Stress that you are not looking for vast amounts of writing and that they should concentrate on carefully selecting the words they use.

Plenary

Listen to several of the children's story extensions. Encourage the others to listen and comment on any powerful verbs they have chosen. Be wary of inconsistent use of tenses.

Assessment

Sentence level

After this unit it is important to ensure that pupils stick with the same tense within a text. They should be able to identify in their own writing when a shift in tense has been made and correct it. Over time they should have their attention drawn to any immature use of past tense (*he doned it*). Draw pupils' attention to incorrect forms.

Writing composition

Pupils should choose powerful speech verbs and use the Reminder Sheet to help set out their new dialogue correctly. When marking insist that this is correct so that the habit becomes established early.

Model answers

Pupils' Book ◻ A

1 *She is worried, nervous, anxious.*
2 Various clues – *Mrs Kane screamed, moaned Mrs Kane, she asks her husband to do something, she whispers, she calls out, 'Dan! Come away this minute'.*
3 *He is amazed, intrigued, fascinated.*
4 *Admiringly*

Pupils' Book ◻ B

5 *moaned, whispered, cried*
6 *Any verb in the past tense from the extract, e.g. jumped, landed, screamed, etc.*
7 *Dan got up and strode over to the mantlepiece.*
   The Gift from Winklesea had hidden behind the clock.

It darted so swiftly that they hardly saw it disappear.
'It's staring at us!'
But she, too, wandered over and joined them.

8 (Draw attention to powerful speech verbs.)
9 went: *ran, hobbled, leaped, darted, dashed, tore ...*
   looked: *stared, glared, gazed, peered at, etc.*

◻ 5A   Matching the feelings 🄿

There are many alternative speech verbs, from which pupils will choose to show the growing fear and tension in the passage. The main thing is that the verbs are appropriate to the tone and feeling of the moment.

◻ 5B   Which verb tense? 🄿

1 *A – present; B – present; C – past*

1 Read this passage, thinking about how each character might be feeling as they speak.
2 Then change each speech verb to match these feelings.

The Voice in the Darkness

'Stop!' said Jake.

Joanna stared at him.

'What's the matter?' she said.

'I thought I heard something,' said Jake.

'I didn't,' said Joanna. But just as she spoke they heard

the sound of footsteps on the path behind them. The

children stared at each other.

'Who's there?' said Jake in a bold voice.

'It's me,' said a voice from out of the darkness.

'Run,' said Jake. He had recognized the voice.

'Noooooo,' said Joanna, as a cold hand grabbed her ankle.

'At last,' said the voice. A voice that spoke with the

coldness of Winter, with the years of loneliness. It was

the voice of hatred.

1 Read each of the four extracts below and decide which tense each one is written in. Write *past* or *present* next to each one.

2 Now rewrite one of the extracts in a different tense in the space below.

A

At night when it is dark and I am in bed and I can't get to sleep I hear noises. I hear tap, tap, tap. I know what it is. It's a tree blowing in the wind. It taps on the glass. That's all. But I like to pretend it's The Flat Man trying to get in. His long, bony finger taps on the glass. 'Let me in,' he whispers. Tap, tap, tap.

From *The Flat Man* (Ragged Bear, 1989), copyright © Rose Impey 1989, reprinted by permission of Mathew Price Children's Books

B

Come on, let's go up to my bedroom. My mum's got visitors coming round and she's having a bit of a spring clean. She only gets the Hoover out once in a blue moon, but when she does – look out! She's dangerous. Dad's in the kitchen making pizza. Do you like pizza? I adore it.

From *The Sleepover Club at Felicity's: quick, the toaster's on fire!* (Collins, 1997), copyright © Rose Impey 1997, reprinted by permission of HarperCollins Publishers, Ltd

C

Hamish Bigmore behaved even worse than they had expected. He found all their favourite books and games, which they tried to hide from him and spoilt them or left them lying about the house where they got trodden on and broken. He pulled the stuffing out of Wim's favourite teddy bear, bounced up and down so hard on the garden frame that it bent and talked for hours and hours after the light had been put out at night, so that Thomas and Pete couldn't get to sleep.

From *Mr Majeika* (Kestrel, 1994), copyright © Humphrey Carpenter 1994, reprinted by permission of Penguin Books Ltd

....

....

....

....

Improving dialogue

Tell the reader how a character thinks and feels by choosing a good speech verb.

'Goodbye,' said Jake.	Tells us nothing about how Jake feels.
'Goodbye,' cheered Jake.	Tells us how pleased Jake feels.

Some good speech verbs:
yell, scream, shout, explode, bellow, call, cry, roar, bawl, holler, thunder, hiss, whine, moan, groan, whimper, whisper, murmur, sigh

Improving sentences in stories

Tell the reader how things happen by choosing powerful verbs.

The man went down the road.	Tells us nothing about how the man moved.
The man hopped down the road.	Creates a stronger picture of how the man moved.

Some powerful verbs instead of 'went':
dart, dash, scurry, jog, scamper, trot, wander, dawdle, idle, crawl, creep, hop, skip, bound, sprint, bolt, scarper, skedaddle

Writing stories

When you are writing a story you can make it happen:

long ago – past tense   *Sam ran down the path.*
now – present tense   *Sam runs down the path.*

Verbs in reports

The purpose of this unit is to help children structure their report writing, using the present tense consistently, as well as deepening their basic understanding of verbs.

NLS coverage

Key objective

SL 3 To reinforce understanding of the function of verbs in sentences
4 To use verb tenses with increasing accuracy in writing and use the present tense in report writing
5 To use the term *verb* appropriately

Learned through:

TL Writing comprehension
22 To write simple non-chronological reports from known information, e.g. from own experiences or from texts read, using notes made to organize and present ideas

Assessment criteria

SL By the end of this unit, pupils should be able to:
- use the term *verb* accurately when discussing reading or writing
- use the correct tense consistently in their own writing
- use the present tense in report writing

TL Writing composition
Pupils should be able to write a simple non-chronological report from notes they have made

Session 1

You will need OHT 6 and PCM 6A.

Shared reading

1 Display OHT 6: *Oakridge Lynch*. (with cross-curricular links to Geography: Study of local area). Explain to pupils that this text is a report on a place – Oakridge Lynch. Read the report through with the class and then take their initial responses.
- Would you like to live in Oakridge Lynch?
- What are the main things that you would enjoy?
- What might be the disadvantages?
- What sort of people would live here?
- How would they earn their living?
- How does this place differ from where you live?

2 Focus on how the report is written. Reread the passage, deciding what each paragraph tells the reader. From this, create a wall chart with simple paragraph headings and summarize the children's ideas. For example:

Paragraph 1: an introduction/tells us what is being written about/it tells us what it is/the definition/the subject.
Paragraph 2: tells us where it is/where it is found/location.
Paragraph 3: tells us what is there/the sorts of buildings you find there/some main places/amenities.
Paragraph 4: tells us what you can do there/interesting things different people do/activities.
Paragraph 5: a conclusion/tells us what people think about the place.

This writing frame may be converted into a reminder sheet or wall chart on how a report can be structured. Reports, whether they are about people, places, creatures, objects, or events, begin with an introduction to what is being written about. This is then followed by the main facts, interesting points, and comments. Sometimes pictures and diagrams may be used to give the reader further information. Reports end with some form of conclusion, often relating the subject back to the reader.

Sentence level work

1 Underline the verbs in the passage and ask pupils what they notice? Explain that the verbs are in the present tense – unlike the past tense verbs from the stories in unit 5. Emphasize that reports are nearly always in the present tense and that stories are usually written in the past tense, though some are in the present tense. Recounts are in the past tense as they record what has already happened.

2 To reinforce the need for present tense, take the opening line: *Oakridge Lynch is a small village.* Ask how the meaning would change if this was written in the past tense, i.e. it would make it sound as if the village did not exist any more. Stress that the only time when the past tense might be used would be when reporting on a past event, person, or place, such as The Romans. Try altering some of the other verbs to the past tense to see how odd it sounds.

Independent activities

Direct pupils to PCM 6A: *Unmuddling a report.* Ask pupils to use the writing frame for reports to cut up and reassemble this passage on London in the correct order. The task's aim is to reinforce the basic structure of a report.

Early finishers could list main advantages and disadvantages of living in their locality, as compared to living in a small village like Oakridge or a city like London.

Plenary

Reinforce the basic structure of a report by running through the writing frame with the class.

Reread PCM 6A and identify verbs in the present tense as a way of reminding pupils of the main verb tense of reports.

Session 2

You will need Pupils' Book Unit 6 pages 16–17 and PCM 6B.

Shared reading

1 Read together the report on *Battle* in the Pupils' Book. Discuss with pupils the kinds of things that they like and dislike about this place.

2 Revisit the writing frame to check whether the report is structured in the same way.

3 Identify differences between your locality and the place described in the report.

Sentence level work

1 Read the report through, identifying the verbs in the present tense. Find the one place where a verb is used in the past tense and ask pupils why it is, i.e. it is about a historical event.

2 Reinforce the need for present tense by changing the verbs in various sentences to the past tense. Ask

children to listen to the effect of this and discuss how it makes it sound as if Battle no longer exists.

Independent activities

Activities A and B in the Pupils' Book explore pupils' basic understanding of the report and focus upon the use of past and present tenses.

Plenary

Listen to pupils' answers, checking that everyone is beginning to understand the difference between past and present tense and their uses in report writing.

Session 3

You will need Pupils' Book Unit 6 pages 16–17 and the Reminder Sheet.

Shared writing

Explain that you are going to write a report about a place you know well. Show the children how the writing frame can be used to prepare for this. Model making brief notes under each heading of details to be included. Avoid choosing your own immediate area for the report, as that will be used for the independent writing activity.

Write together

Demonstrate how to use the plan to write a draft in complete sentences. This is important as many pupils do not know how to move from a plan made with brief notes to creating fluent texts in whole sentences. Draw attention to the need for verbs to keep to the same tense. Introduce the Reminder Sheet as support.

Remember to think aloud, rereading as you write. Involve the children in suggesting ideas and turning your notes into appropriate sentences. You may decide to make several purposeful errors and then show pupils how to reread, spot errors, and improve the text.

Independent writing activity

The shared writing should lead directly to activity C in the Pupils' Book with pupils writing a report about their local area. The first stage is for the children to imitate the process in the shared writing by making notes under the framework headings. They can use PCM 6B. *Writing reports* which is a planning sheet with the headings for each paragraph. Once this is complete, they should write a draft.

To give the activity a specific purpose, explain that their report is for a guidebook about their locality for people who do not know about their area. If you have Internet of e-mail access to reports on your area, pupils' reports could be embellished with pictures and e-mailed to another school.

Plenary

When responding or marking make sure that:

- The writing frame is used
- The report has been written in the present tense consistently

Summarize what has been learned by referring to the Reminder Sheet.

Assessment

Sentence level
Pupils should be able to discuss which tense is suitable for different writing tasks. They should use the term *verb* when discussing their reading and writing.

Writing composition
Pupils should understand the basic structure of a report and be able to apply this to other topic areas.

Model answers

Pupils' Book A

1 *Six miles from the seaside town of Hastings*
2 *The Abbey*
3 *Because it is built on the site of the battle of Hastings*
4 *The firework display and bonfire in the middle of the town on November 5th*

Pupils' Book B

5 *One of the exciting things that you can do in the town.*
6 Has – had; are – were; live – lived
7 *The town is very small.*
   There is a hospital on the edge of town.
   The school has over 100 children.

6A   Unmuddling a report

The correct order for the paragraphs is:

Para 1: *London is a large city.*
Para 2: *London is the capital of England. It is situated …*
Para 3: *The city has about seven million…*
Para 4: *There are lots of things that you can do in the London…*
Para 5: *London is an interesting place to visit.*

The paragraphs in this report have been muddled up. Cut them out and decide which order they should really be in.

London

London is an interesting place to visit.

There are lots of things that you can do in London. Every year people from across the world visit the city. There are many museums to visit. You can see famous shows like *Cats*. The streets are always lively. On Saturdays there are street markets where you can buy all sorts of goods. However, some children do not have any places where they can play. Their parents do not like them playing on the street as they say it is dangerous.

London is the capital of England. It is situated by the River Thames, in the south of England. The city covers many miles.

The city has about seven million people living there. Some of the most famous buildings in the world are in London. The Queen lives at Buckingham Palace. You can see the Houses of Parliament and the Tower of London. One of the tallest buildings in the world is the Post Office Tower. There are many thousands of houses, schools and shops. In the centre of the city there is a famous park, called Regents Park. In the park there is a statue of J M Barry who wrote the famous book about Peter Pan.

London is a large city.

Use this planner to help you make notes for your report.

Report planner

Paragraph 1 – introduction/what is it?

Paragraph 2 – where is it?

Paragraph 3 – what is there?

Paragraph 4 – what can you do there?

Paragraph 5 – conclusion/what is it like to live or visit there?

6 *Verbs in reports*

Report structure

1 Reports are useful because they inform people about a particular subject. They give information.

2 Reports have:
   - An introduction that tells us what is being written about.
   - Paragraphs that add more information and description.
   - A conclusion that usually comments on the subject.

3 You can use illustrations and diagrams to add more information to a report.

Using the present tense in reports

Reports are written in the present tense, except when they are about things that happened long ago.

Question & exclamation marks

The purpose of this unit is to allow pupils to look at the importance of punctuation, through reading, and to begin to use these aspects of punctuation in their own writing.

NLS coverage

Key objective

SL 2 To take account of the grammar and punctuation, e.g. sentences, speech marks, exclamation marks and commas to mark pauses, when reading aloud
6 To secure knowledge of question marks and exclamation marks in reading, understand their purpose and use appropriately in own writing

Learned through:

TL Reading comprehension
4 To read, prepare, and present playscripts
5 To recognize the key differences between prose and playscript, e.g. by looking at dialogue, stage directions, layout of text in prose, and playscripts

TL Writing composition
10 Using reading as a model, to write own passages of dialogue
14 To write simple playscripts based on own reading and oral work

Assessment criteria

SL By the end of this unit, pupils should be able to:
■ read with expression appropriate to the grammar and punctuation of a text
■ use question marks and exclamation marks in writing

TL Writing composition
Pupils should be able to write dialogue within a simple playscript format

Session 1

You will need OHT 7 and PCM 7A.

Shared reading

1 Explain to children that you are going to read a playscript. Ask them if they have read any playscripts before? Discuss the different purposes of narrative and script. Then build up a list of situations where scripts are used, e.g. plays, pantomimes, speeches, TV programmes, films, etc.

2 Display OHT 7: *Late Again* but reveal only the setting text. Discuss the possibilities for the script. What might the characters be like? What might normally happen in the hall in the morning?

3 Read the rest of the text with the class and take their initial reactions. Encourage pupils to say if they recognize the scene from their own experience.
   ■ What is the relationship between the three characters in this passage?
   ■ Can you find clues in the script to support this view?
   ■ How would you describe the moods of the three characters?
   ■ Again, can you find clues in the script to support this view?
   ■ What do you think might happen next?

4 Discuss the layout of the playscript, highlighting the characters' names, explicit dialogue, setting text, and stage directions. Ask pupils for differences between playscript and narrative layout and make a class list of these that might be used as a wall chart.

Sentence level work

1 Following on from the discussion about characters' feelings, look again at the text. Explain that there are a number of text features that lead the reader to these conclusions about the characters. First of all, there are the words, which reveal a lot. Then there is the punctuation used by the writer, which emphasizes the meaning of the words. This is more

important in some sentences than others. Offer these examples:

What'll the battleaxe say?

Got any sellotape?

The reader can tell these are both questions from the punctuation and the order of the words.

We're fed up too – with you!

Helen!

The reader knows that these are exclamations because of the punctuation – and partly from the words themselves!

2 Seek volunteers for reading the scene and practise reading the parts, paying particular attention to the punctuation. Ask pupils to read without expression. This is not as easy as it sounds!

Discuss with the children the impact of the punctuation. Remind them how well it emphasizes the meaning of the words – it actually adds to the meaning.

Independent activities

PCM 7A: *Bringing out meaning* is Scene 2 of the script. However, only basic punctuation has been used here: full stops and capital letters. Pupils' task is to read the text in pairs and decide on more effective punctuation to bring out the meaning, in particular through questions marks and exclamation marks.

Plenary

Listen to pupils' alternative readings of Scenes 1 and 2. Encourage the rest of the class to comment. Discuss pupils' use of punctuation in PCM 7A and summarize the punctuation that pairs agree and disagree on. Draw out the meanings created by different ways of punctuating Scene 2.

Session 2

You will need Pupils' Book Unit 7 pages 18–19 and PCM 7B.

Shared reading

1 Explain to pupils that you are going to read another playscript in the form of *Going Bowling* from the Pupils' Book. Tell them that this time the setting is a bowling alley and that they will learn more about this setting as they read through the playscript.

2 Tell children that they have five minutes to read the playscript to themselves and find out why the characters are at the bowling alley. If they find out

quickly, they should check with the pupil next to them.

3 Allow time for reading and then take responses from the pupils, especially about the moods of the characters.

■ Why are the characters at the bowling alley?

■ Are they all enjoying themselves?

■ Which child is not happy?

■ Why is that? Look for clues in the text.

4 Review the features of playscript as discussed in Session 1.

Sentence level work

1 Link back to the characters' moods by looking closely at the information in the text which allows us to gauge the mood of each one. Once again, pupils should focus on:

■ Word choice

■ Word order

■ Punctuation

Invite individuals to read a script part, using expression to convey their character's feelings. Each time, stress how the writer lets the reader know about how the character is feeling.

2 Discuss the use of question marks and exclamation marks in *Going Bowling*. Which of these punctuation marks is easier to use and interpret? Read the questions together and notice how the inflection of the voice changes at the end of a question.

Now look at the first two exclamations. There is still a lot of interpretation to be done here. Exclamation marks can indicate a range of different emotions. Talk over the first two instances and ask what they are expressing, e.g the first one indicates satisfaction. This will lead directly into activity B in the Pupils' Book.

Independent activities

Activity A in the Pupils' Book reinforces the discussion of the characters' moods in *Going Bowling* and can be used in conjunction with PCM 7B: *Showing moods*. In activity B, pupils continue the task of nominating an emotion for each exclamation in the script.

Plenary

Ask pupils to share their views on where Mel goes and why.

Gather feedback on activity B and provide some examples from pupils' current reading books, which use exclamation marks and discuss their use.

Sum up by making sure that children understand that they must attend to word choice, word order, and punctuation when reading aloud and when inferring about characters' feelings.

Session 3

You will need Pupils' Book Unit 7 pages 18–19 and the Reminder Sheet.

Shared writing

1 Explain to pupils that you are going to write a playscript version of a text which is familiar to them from shared reading. Work only on a short extract as there will be a lot of discussion. You will probably write less than you expect!

2 Remind children of the layout of a playscript – refer back to model texts and to the wall chart from Session 1. Now look at the text on which you are basing the script. Using an enlarged version or an OHT, lay an acetate sheet over the text and invite pupils to highlight the dialogue in the text.

Write together

1 Begin to write the script onto a OHT or flipchart. Start with the setting. Discuss what is known about the setting. Is there anything else which pupils can work out about it from the extract?

2 Next start to convert a section of dialogue into script. Model script layout, referring back to model texts. Remind children that speech punctuation is not necessary in a script. Discuss what should be included in the dialogue. Given that there will be no narrative, is there any detail from the original text that should be built into the dialogue? Consider choice of words and punctuation.

3 Continue to write, focusing on choice of words and punctuation to emphasize feelings and expression.

Independent writing activity

Pupils may be given the choice to either continue *Going Bowling* from the Pupils' Book, as part of activity C or to write a playscript based on a text of their choice. Guide pupils to an appropriate choice of text if they take the latter option.

Plenary

Ask pupils to hand their playscript to others to rehearse and read aloud. The readers should have an opportunity to comment on how much support there is in the text for expression.

Assessment

Sentence level
Pupils should be able to use question marks and exclamation marks in their writing. They should understand their function in sentences and their meaning when reading with expression.

Writing composition
Pupils should be familiar with simple playscript format and be able to write a continuation of a known script.

Model answers

Pupils' Book ▱ A
1 *It is Mel's birthday.*
2 *She has missed the pins.*
3 *He thinks it's funny.*
4 *She's probably just gone home / run off / etc.*
5 *It's her birthday, and no one is taking any notice of her.*

Pupils' Book ▱ B
6 *Go on then – better that!*   *(James – proud)*
  Boys!   *(Mel – sneering / disdainful)*
  Girls!   *(James – scornful)*

▱7A   Bringing out meaning ▣
There is a lot of room for manoeuvre on this PCM, particularly for use of exclamation marks. You may wish to discuss the number of exclamation marks used at a guided reading/writing session.

▱7B   Showing moods ▣
Comment on the extent to which pupils have selected appropriate vocabulary, and on the alterations they have made. Less able pupils may only complete the first part of the task.

7A **Bringing out meaning**

In Scene 2 of the playscript, the writer has only used capital letters and full stops.

1 Read the playscript in pairs. Then decide together where to put question marks and exclamation marks to bring out the full meaning.

2 When you have finished, practise reading this part of the script as you have punctuated it.

Scene 2: Simon's idea

Setting: at the school gates, 8.15 am

Helen: Oh, great. School isn't even open yet. I knew we'd be too early. Who said we had to be here this early.

Ben: There you go again. Whinge, whinge, mutter, mutter... . Can't you hear yourself, Helen. Ms Trott will be here any minute now. Just be patient.

Helen: I'm sorry, I'm cold and tired. I don't even belong to the choir. I just have to stand around waiting for Lynn to come in.

Simon: Hey – I've got an idea. Why don't you join the choir. Lynn could join too – she likes singing. Then you'd be in the warm with us. Here's Ms Trott now – let's ask her.

7B Showing moods

Use this chart to record the moods of James, Charlotte and Mel in *Going Bowling*. Show which comments and punctuation marks help you to tell how they feel in column three.

Character	Mood	How I know
James		
Charlotte		
Mel		

Playscript layout

Playscripts are set out differently from stories. They are written to be read aloud by different people.

- Start with a description of the setting (where everything happens).
- Write the name of the character who is speaking at the start of the line.
- Write the words they say after a space.
- Remember that you don't need speech marks.

  For example:

> **Charlotte:** Sorry, Mel. I just know I'm better than him. I always win. I'm going to have another go.

Using questions and exclamation marks in playscripts

When you write a playscript, it is very important to help readers work out how the characters are feeling and talking. There are two things to think about:

- Word choice: think carefully about the words you choose, so that readers will know how characters are feeling.
- Punctuation: use question marks and exclamation marks to help readers.

  For example:

> **James:** Yes! Go on then... better that!
> and
> **Charlotte:** James – where's Mel?

UNIT 8 *Using nouns*

The purpose of this unit is to introduce nouns. Once children understand the basic concept of nouns as words that name something or somebody in a sentence, they can consider their choice of nouns. They should be aware of the need to choose specific nouns, for instance, *vulture* or *robin* rather than *bird*.

NLS coverage

Key objective

SL To understand the function of nouns within sentences by:
- identifying them in shared reading
- noticing that if nouns are removed from a sentence it will no longer make sense
- identifying and using specific nouns to create stronger pictures in the reader's mind, e.g. *dalmatian* or *poodle* rather than *dog*

Learned through:

TL Reading comprehension
4 To choose and prepare poems for performance, identifying appropriate expression, tone, volume and use of voices and other sounds
8 To rehearse and improve performance, taking note of punctuation and meaning

WL W17 To generate synonyms for high-frequency words

TL Writing composition
11 To write new or extended verses for performance based on models of 'performance' and oral poetry reading, e.g. rhythms, repetition

Assessment criteria

SL By the end of this unit, pupils should be able to:
- identify a noun in a sentence
- explain that a noun stands for something or somebody
- notice when a noun might be made more specific and think of alternatives

TL Writing composition
Pupils should be able to write an extension to a poem, using repetitive phrases ...

Session 1

You will need OHT 8 and PCM 8A.

Shared reading

1 Start the session by explaining that you are going to look at the words in sentences that are nouns.

2 Show OHT 8: *What do you see?* and begin the session by listing various nouns from the classroom. Introduce the idea that nouns are like labels that tell us the name of something or somebody.

Sentence level work

1 Move on to read the poem on OHT 8 that begins *From my window…*. Ask pupils which are the nouns – what does the cat see? Underline the nouns, e.g. *dog, cat, man.*

2 Encourage pupils to look carefully for other nouns – *road, seat, flower, tree*, etc. What do they notice about the preceding words? Usually nouns can be preceded by *a, an,* or *the*.

3 Now reread the poem – are the pictures that the sentences make effective? Are some of them rather dull? Explain that some of the nouns could be improved by 'naming' them, i.e. being more exact or precise. For instance, just to write *dog* does not give the reader much of a clue – what colour, what sort? Ask if anyone can think of a better alternative? Take some ideas from pupils, e.g. *Rottweiler, sausage dog, poodle*, etc. Again *road* does not tell the reader much about the road. However, *Gloucester High Street* creates a definite picture for the reader.

4 Read through the poem and change more of the nouns for specific (though the milkman and moon sentences you may decide to leave as they are).

Independent activities

Use PCM 8A: *Using stronger nouns*. Read the poem through with pupils. Explain that it is a draft. Their task is to underline all the nouns. Then they decide whether any of them could be changed to make stronger pictures and write in the alternatives.

Plenary

Listen to pupils' ideas for redrafting the poem in PCM 8A. Ensure that they have underlined all the nouns and check whether there are any misconceptions. Discuss possible alternatives and what these infer. For instance, a word like Rottweiler means a large, savage dog to me – whereas an Old English Terrier would be soppy. Each noun holds different layers of meaning for the reader, depending on their experience.

Reread the original poem from PCM 8A alongside a version that contains more lively nouns, so pupils can hear the difference. End the session by summarizing with the pupils what they now know about nouns – what they are and the need to select them with care.

Session 2

You will need Pupils' Book Unit 8 pages 20–21 and PCM 8B.

Shared reading

1 Read the first two lines of the poem, *Cat in the Window* in the Pupils' Book and pause. Ask pupils, *What might a cat see from a window?* Take a number of ideas from the children.

2 Read the whole poem through several times with the children joining in. Then explore pupils' reactions through these questions.
   ■ What time of year is it – which words suggest it?
   ■ Find three things the cat can see.
   ■ How would you feel outside?
   ■ Find the pattern – basic line structure and rhyme.

3 Read the poem through again. This time split pupils into groups, each reading a different verse.

Sentence level work

1 Take the first two verses in turn and decide which words are the nouns. List whatever the cat can see – this will help pupils to focus upon collecting nouns.

2 Take a closer look at the poet's name. Make the point that names of people and places are special; therefore they start with a capital letter. Check the names of the other authors in this book. In forthcoming sessions be on the lookout for other instances of proper nouns being identifiable by starting with a capital letter. This idea is returned to in the Unit 10 *Capital letters*.

Independent activities

Activity A provides a few questions about the poem which focus pupils on strong visual cues in the text. In activity B pupils have to list 15 nouns from the poem. They also have to improve the nouns *cat*, *bird*, and *tree*. Remind the children that they are changing these nouns to improve the picture in the reader's mind.

PCM 8B: *Nonsense nouns* is a cloze procedure where all the nouns have been replaced by nonsense words. This will be useful for pupils who are still struggling with the concept. They have to replace the nonsense word with a sensible noun.

Plenary

Hear all the nouns the children have found and take different suggestions for strengthening verses 1 and 2. Reread the poem's opening with different nouns to see what sort of effect can be created. Try to use nouns that create a different atmosphere, e.g. comforting (*Siamese*, *robin*, *Christmas tree*) or something frightening (*tiger*, *vulture*, *acacia tree*).

Session 3

You will need Pupils' Book Unit 8 pages 20–21 and the Reminder Sheet.

Shared writing

1 Explain that you are going to write a poem together based on *Cat in the Window*, and reread the poem.

2 Take a moment just to check the form of the poem. Notice the opening two lines – this can be replicated for another cat, a dog, a budgie, a person, a cow from a stall, a tiger from a cage, a postman from his van, a pilot from a plane... List a number of possible ideas for the opening and agree upon one. Keep it simple.

Write together

1 Having decided on the opening lines, let us say *Bus conductor in your bus/what do you see?*, brainstorm a list of nouns that the conductor might see. (Lamppost, statue, car, trees, etc.) You need only 6–8 ideas.

2 Revisit the list to see which nouns could be made stronger – a statue of whom? What is the name of the shop? What sort of car? Try to make the list particular to your area – otherwise you end up with bland nouns and you could be writing about anywhere, anytime.

3 Now demonstrate how to take a noun and extend the sentence. For instance:

Bus conductor from your bus
What do you see?

A lamppost standing alone
Like a ship's mast lost.

A statue of Prince Albert
Staring across the forgotten streets.

A Mercedes glides by,
Silent as a ghost.

Fir trees rustling their skirts
At the edge of Cirencester...

4 Before the children begin work on their own poem for activity C, they should work in pairs and decide on their opening two lines. The next stage is to brainstorm their list of nouns with their partners and then improve them. Have some read aloud. See if any could be improved.

Independent writing activity

Ensure every child has written their opening two lines of their poem for activity C and listed the nouns they are going to write about. Encourage them to work silently and swiftly, concentrating on the flow of ideas.

Plenary

Listen to pupils' poems. Draw attention to ideas that are imaginative, to effective use of language, and to nouns that are very specific and therefore create a strong picture.

If there are examples of nouns used that might be improved, reread the line to see if the pupils can spot which word needs changing. Let them generate a range of alternatives but leave the decision with the writer.

As pupils read their work aloud, comment on how effective their readings are. End this unit of work by summarizing with pupils what they have learned about nouns. The key points are on the Reminder Sheet.

Assessment

Sentence level
Pupils should know that a noun names something or somebody and be able to identify nouns in sentences; they should also be able to spot weak nouns; and be able to think of more specific examples.

Writing composition
Mark weak nouns in pupils' poems to encourage them to be specific in their choice. Children should be able to take a simple structure from a poem and add further lines or verses.

Model answers

Pupils' Book ☐ A

1 *Shivering*

2 *The word 'dusk' suggests that it might be just before night-time. However, the poet might be suggesting that the cloud is so dark that it makes it look like dusk.*

3 *The daffodils shivering in the February breeze, the puddle freezing, snow on the wind, dusk in a cloud, leaves in a frenzy and the cowed bird's head.*

4 Various answers, e.g. *The cat feels cosy because it is in the warm whilst outside it is cold and wintry.*

Pupils' Book ☐ B

5 *Cat, window, cloud, leaves, bird, tree, daffodils, puddle, road, snow, wind, dusk, frenzy, head, winter, sun, blizzard*

6 Cat: *Siamese, Burmese, tabby, etc.*
Bird: *hawk, robin, thrush, linnet, etc.*
Tree: *fir, oak, elm, ash, sapling, etc.*

7 Answers might include – *houses, cars, railings, etc.*

☐8A Using stronger nouns P

1 Nouns – *dreams, fish, river, car, road, piece, fruit, plate, field, vegetables, animal, cage, boy shop*

2 When rewriting, pupils should select more precise nouns, e.g.
In my dreams I saw –
A trout swimming in the River Thames,

3 Encourage the use of precise nouns.

☐8B Nonsense nouns P

Answers that reflect the specific noun type suggested by the nonsense word should be given special credit, e.g.
A Rottweiler barks angrily at a postman.

8A *Using stronger nouns*

1 Read the poem and underline all the nouns.

2 Change any nouns that you think could be made stronger.

3 Write several more lines to the poem. Remember to choose your nouns with care so that they make a strong picture in the reader's mind.

> In my dreams I saw –
>
> a fish swimming in the river,
>
> a car speeding down the road,
>
> a piece of fruit on a white plate,
>
> a field of vegetables,
>
> an animal in a cage,
>
> a boy standing outside a shop.
>
> ....
>
> ....
>
> ....
>
> ....

Read the poem. Some of the nouns have been replaced by a nonsense word.
Change the nouns for something specific.

In the park I watch and wonder –

 Just what is that?

A flitcher barks angrily at a postman.

Two tranchlings peck at a packet of crisps.

A purdgy swims across the lake, her white wings folded.

From the swings Poggle screams with delight.

A borrogot trundles past, down the street.

What is a noun?

A noun is a word that names something or somebody. It can often be preceded by *a*, *an* or *the*.

> *I saw a dog eating a bone.*
>
> In this sentence *dog* and *bone* are nouns.

Choosing nouns

When you are writing, it is important to make sure that you choose your nouns with care so that you make a strong picture in the reader's mind. For instance, in the sentence:

> *The dog came up to me.*
>
> The noun *dog* is not well chosen. Is it a Rottweiler or a poodle?

When you are writing a red alarm should sound whenever you use any of these words – because usually you can find a more precise word.

boy	cat
girl	animal
man	insect
woman	fish
tree	car
bird	street
dog	town

Singular & plural nouns

The purpose of this unit is to introduce and explore the idea of singular and plural.
It links strongly to accurate spelling within sentences.

NLS coverage

Key objective

SL 4 To extend knowledge of pluralization through:
- recognizing the use of singular and plural forms in speech and through shared reading
- transforming sentences from singular to plural and vice versa, noting which words have to change and which do not
- understanding the term *collective noun* and collecting examples – experiment with inventing other collective nouns
- noticing which nouns can be pluralized and which cannot, e.g. rain
- recognizing pluralization as one test of a noun

5 To use the terms singular and plural appropriately

Learned through:

TL **Writing composition**
10 To write alternative sequels to traditional stories using same characters and settings, identifying typical phrases and expressions from the story and using these to help structure the writing

WL To investigate and identify basic rules for changing the spelling of nouns when *s* is added

Assessment criteria

SL By the end of this unit, pupils should be able to:
- transform sentences from singular to plural
- use the terms singular and plural appropriately
- understand the common spelling patterns for most plurals

TL **Writing composition**
Pupils should be able to write an alternative sequel to a traditional story using same characters and settings and identifying typical phrases from the original tale

Session 1

You will need OHT 9 and PCM 9A.

Shared reading

1 Display OHT 9: *The Stranger and the Cooking Pot.* Cover the main text and read the sentences at the top of OHT 9. Use a pen to transform these sentences from singular to plural. Label each sentence for pupils, making the point that when there is only *one* then the noun is singular, if there are *two* or more then the noun is in the plural. Explain that generally this means adding an *s*, though some plurals are spelt differently.

2 If you need to demonstrate the difference between singular and plural, give examples from objects around the room.

3 Read the main text and discuss the following to gauge pupils' initial reactions.
- Name two things we know about the stranger.
- What woke the stranger up – what does that tell us about how the stranger felt?
- Find any words or phrases that are typical of traditional tales. (e.g. *he was so hungry that...* repeated three times).

Sentence level work

1 Reread the text through and then transform all the nouns from singular to plural, so that there are lots

of old men, old women, and strangers! Demonstrate how to reread to check for sense and show that some words do not need to be spelt differently or the sentence adjusted.

2 Begin a chart to show how different words change their spelling when they become plural. Which words add an 's', which change 'y' to 'ies', which change 'f' to 'ves', which words do not change, which words add on 'es' rather than 's' and so on. This chart should be displayed and added to during the course of this unit, to establish some basic rules for spelling plural words.

Independent activities

Direct pupils to PCM 9A: *Singular to plural*. Read the text through several times. Explain that it features Jack from *Jack and the Beanstalk* and that there are many traditional tales based on this character.

Pupils' task is to transform the nouns into plural, thinking about spelling and whether any other words, such as verbs, need to be altered.

Plenary

Listen to pupils' transformations and add any new spellings to the chart. Discuss whether patterns are emerging. It should be possible to get pupils generating some rules.

Session 2

You will need Pupils' Book Unit 9 pages 22–23 and PCM 9B.

Shared reading

1 Turn to *Jack and the Wily Fox* in the Pupils' Book. Read the text through several times, perhaps using volunteers on the second reading to take the spoken parts. Then take pupils' initial reactions.
 - When does the story take place?
 - How does it differ from Jack and the Beanstalk?
 - Why do you think Jack's mother tells him not to swap the animals for beans?
 - What is the silliest thing that Jack does?
 - Is Jack bad?
 - Is there anything that is puzzling about the tale?

2 Reread the text and identify words and phrases that are typical of traditional and oral tales. List these as they may be useful for children's own writing (e.g. *it was not long after, and this time, so off goes Jack, well sooner rather than later,* etc.).

Sentence level work

Focus upon the first nine lines of *Jack and the Wily Fox* and begin to categorize the more obvious nouns according to their endings. Encourage children to articulate possible rules, e.g. it ends in a *y* (*city*) so it probably will be *cities*.

Independent activities

Using PCM 9B: *Singular & plural endings*, the task in activity B is to complete the grid so that there are at least three examples from the story in each column. Some pupils may wish to fill in more if there is time. A dictionary or spelling journal may be useful for double checking entries.

However, once they have three in each column they should transform what Jack says to his mother when he gets back from the market, so that the plurals become singular – with the correct spelling. Of course, they will have to decide independently what to do with the collective nouns.

Plenary

Use the plenary to reinforce the following points about spelling plurals, building on work from Session 1.
 - For most plurals add 's' to the singular.
 - For most words ending in 'ch', 'sh', 'ss' and 'x', add 'es'.
 - For most words ending in 'y', change the 'y' to 'ies'.
 - For most words ending in 'f', change the 'f' to 'ves'.
 - Some words stay the same, e.g. 'sheep'.

Discuss the notion of collective nouns with the children – list any others that they know (e.g. *a school of children, an army of soldiers, a flock of birds, a pack of wolves, a forest of trees,* etc.). If there is time, invent some new ones (e.g. *a storm of footballers, a daintiness of ballet dancers, a business of starlings,* etc.).

Session 3

You will need Pupils' Book Unit 9 pages 22–23 and the Reminder Sheet.

Shared writing

Explain that you are going to write another Jack story. In the story he gets sent again to the market. What could happen this time? Take a range of suggestions. For example: he could meet someone on the way; he could be distracted and never get there; he could buy the wrong thing, lose his purchases on the way home, or trade them. The possibilities are endless.

Write together

Begin to compose a version of the tale. Pay particular attention to the nouns, explaining whether they are in the singular or plural. Draw upon spelling rules from the previous sessions to justify spelling of plurals.

In your writing, use the language of traditional tales and bear in mind that events often happen in threes.

Independent writing activity

Following on from the shared writing, pupils can either continue the version that you have begun or pursue their own idea for a new Jack story as part of activity C in the Pupils' Book. Use the Reminder Sheet to secure the spelling of any plurals. Encourage pupils to limit their writing so that the stories remain fairly simple.

Plenary

Listen to several tales. Comment on the originality of the ideas, the use of traditional language, and pick up on examples of nouns that are either singular or plural.

Add to the wall chart for spelling plurals any new examples that fit in.

Assessment

Sentence level
Pupils should be able to use the terms singular and plural accurately in discussion. They should be able to identify singular and plural nouns and discuss possible spellings based on similar instances.
They should be used to transforming sentences from singular to plural or vice versa taking account of any changes needed.

Writing composition
Pupils should be using the language of traditional tales and common motifs within their own story writing.

Model answers

Pupils' Book ☐ A

1 *It's quite a bargain!*

2 2 reasons from these possibilities, e.g. *He is pleased to have bought the animal;, he is pleased to be coming home; he thinks his mother will be pleased with him; he is pleased that he did not swap them for something silly, etc.*

3 *The fox is hungry, as it says 'the temptation got too much'.*

4 *She will tell him that he is silly for putting animals together that are going to fight or try to eat each other!*

5 Various possible ideas, e.g. *Do not swap the animals for anything silly. Only buy cows, pigs, sheep and horses, etc.*

Pupils' Book ☐ B

6 giant – giants   city – cities   wolf – wolves
fish – fishes   beanstalk – beanstalks   sky – skies
roof – rooves   lunch – lunches   garden – gardens
fly – flies   leaf – leaves   fox – foxes
sheep – sheep   goose – geese
swarm of bees   pride of lions   herd of cattle

7 *'Here you are mother, I've brought one of each animal I saw at the market, as well as some I collected on the way. I've got a dog, cat, horse, fox, fish, fly, duck, goose, chicken, bunny, wolf, sheep, bee, lion, and a cow.'*

☐9A Singular to plural ⊡

The rewritten passage should read something like this:
On the <u>tables</u> lay <u>several</u> bright new <u>pennies</u>, <u>some</u> old <u>teeth</u>, <u>mice</u> and <u>dice</u>. Jack picked them up and put everything into his <u>sacks</u>. He slung the <u>sacks</u> onto the <u>carts</u> beside the <u>sacks</u> of magic corn. He spoke several <u>words</u> into the horses' <u>ears</u> and away they went.

No sooner had they left the <u>towns</u> than the old <u>teeth</u> bit their way through the <u>sacks</u>. The <u>mice</u> nibbled through the <u>sacks</u> of corn.

Jack noticed some <u>beggars</u> at the side of the <u>roads</u>. He stopped for some <u>games</u>. He bet the <u>men</u> his bright <u>pennies</u>. They rolled the dice to see who would win. Each time Jack rolled the dice he won. He won gold <u>cups</u>, wooden <u>boxes</u>, <u>sandwiches</u>, <u>beans</u>, <u>brushes</u>, <u>shoes</u> and young <u>puppies</u>.

Change this 'Jack' story from singular to plural.

Jack and the Dice

On the table lay one bright new penny, an old tooth, a mouse and a dice.

Jack picked them up and put everything into his sack. He slung the sack onto the cart beside the sack of magic corn. He spoke one word into the horse's ear and away they went.

No sooner had they left the town than the old tooth bit its way through the sack. The mouse nibbled through the sack of corn.

Jack noticed a beggar at the side of the road. He stopped for a game. He bet the man his one bright penny. They rolled the dice to see who would win. Each time Jack rolled the dice he won. He won a gold cup, a wooden box, a sandwich, a bean, a brush, a shoe and a young puppy.

9B Singular & plural endings

Use this grid to collect examples of different plural nouns.

Adds 's'	
Adds 'es'	
Changes to 'ies'	
Changes to 'ves'	
Collective nouns	
No change	
Odd plurals	

9 Singular & plural nouns

1 A noun is singular when there is only one, e.g. *dog*.

2 A noun is plural when there is more than one, e.g. *dogs*.

3 Plural nouns usually have an 's' on the end.
   cat – cats

Other patterns for plural endings.
- Add 'es' if the word ends in 'ss', 'sh' or 'x'.
  moss – mosses, fish – fishes, fox – foxes
- Add 's' to words that end in 'y' if the last letter has a vowel before it.
  donkey – donkeys
- Change the 'y' to an 'i' and add 'es' for other words that end in 'y'.
  city – cities
- Add 's' to words that end in 'ff'.
  cuff – cuffs
- Some words remain the same.
  deer – deer
- Some words change in other ways.
  mouse – mice
- A collective noun is a word that refers to a group.
  crowd, flock, school, team

4 If you can turn a word into a plural, then it is a noun.

5 If you change a word from singular to plural in a sentence you may have to change the spelling of other words.
   The dog runs down the lane.
   The dogs run down the lane.

Capital letters

The purpose of this unit is to investigate in reading the full range of uses for capital letters and begin to use this in their own writing. The vehicle for exploring capital letters is writing instructions, so that by the end of the unit pupils will also be familiar with the basic structure and some language features of instructional texts.

NLS coverage

Key objective

SL 8 To understand the other uses of capitalization from reading, e.g. names, headings, special emphasis, new lines in poetry

Learned through:

TL Reading comprehension

12 To identify the different purposes of instructional texts, e.g. recipes, route-finders ...

13 To discuss the merits and limitations of particular instructional texts, including IT and other media texts, and to compare these with others to give an overall evaluation

14 To discuss how written instructions are organized, e.g. lists, numbered points, diagrams with arrows, bullet points, keys

15 To read and follow simple instructions

TL Writing composition

16 To write instructions, e.g. rules for playing games, recipes, using a range of organizational devices, e.g. lists, dashes, commas for lists in sentences ...

Assessment criteria

SL By the end of this unit, pupils should be able to:
- identify and have begun to use capital letters for a broad range of appropriate purposes
- be able to use a writing frame to write a set of instructions

TL Writing composition
Pupils should be able to write instructions, using a range of organizational devices

Session 1

You will need OHT 10 and PCM 10A.

Shared reading

1 Show OHT 10: *How to make a kite*. What sort of text is this? How do you know? Read the text through with the class and then list the clues that give away that it is a set of instructions, using their ideas. Do not worry if at this stage they do not identify every aspect.

2 Discuss the following.
- Who might read this type of text?
- In which parts of the text is the author trying to persuade the reader to make a kite and fly it?
- Could the the instructions be improved in any way?

3 Explain that you are going to create a writing frame with the class for writing instructions, based on this example. Read the text through with the class again and ask them to help by suggesting the purpose of

each part of the text. This should produce something like this. (Points in brackets refer to language features that you may want to draw out.)
- Title. (Use *How To* to introduce what the instructions will help the reader do.)
- Introduction to instructions. (Explain who might need to follow the instructions and how they might help the reader. You may want to try to convince the reader to use the instructions.)
- List of what is needed. (Use a colon before the list. Use bullet points. List the equipment in the order it is needed.)
- List what to do. (Again, use a colon and bullet points. Notice where the verbs lie at the start of the sentences – *bossy* or imperative verbs that tell the reader what to do. Spend sometime giving orders to reinforce this notion, revisit this in P.E. by using imperative verbs for instructions such as, *Run to the end of the hall.*, etc.)
- End paragraph – testing the end result. (You can add in extra information and/or encourage the reader to have a go at using the instructions.)

Sentence level work

1 Revisit OHT 10. Focus upon the different uses of capital letters. Ask pupils for the main use of capitals.

2 Reread the text, underlining the different places where capital letters are used. Take the children's ideas and list these. Continue to add to this list during the unit and for the rest of the term. It can also be used alongside the Reminder Sheet as an *aide memoire* for pupils during their own writing.

Independent activities

Direct pupils to PCM 10A: *Muddled instructions*. This activity has two parts to it. Explain that your computer has muddled the order of a set of instructions. The task is to put the different sections into the correct order. This can be done by cutting up PCM 10A, and rearranging the sections on another sheet. Alternatively, pupils may simply number each section.

The computer has also missed out all the capital letters. The task is to read through the text and decide where capital letters should be used. Remind the children to use the *reminder* list they have created.

Plenary

Check that pupils have PCM 10A reorganized into the correct order. Read the text through and ask pupils to indicate where they think a capital letter might have been used. The hardest part of this task is for the children to decide whether any words might be emphasized. Are there any new categories to add to the *reminder* list (e.g. title of book/film)?

Show the OHT again and ask if there were any differences – the key one being the use of the alphabet to order the instructions.

Session 2

You will need Pupils' Book Unit 10 pages 24–25 and PCM 10B.

Shared reading

1 Before reading *Wonka's Nutty Crunch Surprise* in the Pupils' Book, tune the children in to the text by revisiting what they know about instructions from Session 1. Find out about their favourite foods, who cooks for them, and what recipes they know.

2 Read *Wonka's Nutty Crunch Surprise* through as a class, several times and take pupils' initial responses.
   - What kind of book does this come from – and where would you find that book?
   - Who might use the book?

- What did the author need to know before writing this?
- Has the writer stuck to the framework for writing?
- Would you know how to go about making *Nutty Crunch Surprise* from this recipe?
- If not what would you want to ask the writer?
- Look at where the recipe is taken from, who wrote the original book, where was it published, and by whom?

Sentence level work

1 Referring to the last question in activity A in the Pupils' Book, discuss different ways to list ingredients, i.e. using the alphabet, numbers, and bullet points. Draw pupils' attention to the use of the colon to introduce a list. Discuss how the writer has used italics for ingredients.

2 Read through the steps needed to cook the recipe and check where the verbs are. Are they *bossy* verbs, that tell the reader what to do?

3 Spend a short time looking at a few instances where capital letters are used to link with activity B. Model how pupils should set out the list in their books:

Word with a capital	Reason for a capital letter
Charlie	It's someone's name.

4 Locate an instance of a capital letter being used for a different reason in another extract from the Pupils' Book. Model how to add this to the list, including the page number in a third column. The challenge of this task in activity B is to see who can find the largest number of different reasons for using a capital letter.

Independent activities

With the initial support given above, all pupils should be able to attempt activities A and B in the Pupil's Book.

PCM .10B: *Choosing the best instructions* offers two examples of instructions. The task is for pupils to decide which is written most effectively. Then they rewrite the poor version, improving it. This activity could be used for early finishers or more skilful writers.

Plenary

List together the reasons for using a capital letter, making a class wall chart. This can be referred to in future lessons. Make it clear that you now expect children to be beginning to use capital letters for the identified reasons.

Model the range of usage in shared writing.

Session 3

You will need Pupils' Book Unit 10 pages 24–25 and the Reminder Sheet.

Shared writing

1 Explain to pupils that you are going to write together a set of instructions for a familiar playground game. Reread the recipe and revisit the main features of instructional texts. Make the point that they can choose whether to use bullet points, numbers or letters as different types of instruction may be best served by slightly different formats.
2 Double check that everyone is familiar with the different uses of capital letters discovered so far.
3 Introduce the writing frame created in Session 1 plus the Reminder Sheet for capital letters.

Write together

1 Agree with the children which playground game might appeal to a younger group.
2 As you compose on a whiteboard, OHT or flipchart, use the writing frame to help structure the text. Think aloud as you are composing, explicitly explaining each aspect.
3 Make sure that you highlight every time that you use a capital letter. This has to become automatic.
4 Keep checking the flow of the text by rereading.

Independent writing activity

Following on from this shared writing, pupils should write their own set of instructions as part of activity C in the Pupils' Book. These instructions will be for a different playground game, based on the writing frame they have just seen you compose. Before they begin, discuss which games might be suitable.

Plenary

The key test of a set of instructions is whether or not they actually work. Therefore a fun way to end this session would be to take one or two sets and see whether, by following exactly what is written, a group can actually play the game.

To focus upon capital letters you will need to make an OHT/flipchart of several examples and use these to begin the next session.

Assessment

Sentence level
Pupils should be able to identify capital letters in a text and suggest reasons for different usages. Increasingly, they should use capital letters as a matter of habit.

Writing composition
Pupils should understand and use a basic writing frame to write a set of instructions. They should begin to manipulate the basic features of an instructional text – headings, colon, bullet points, letters or numbers, sequencing, imperative verbs, temporal connectives such as *first, next, finally*.

Model answers

Pupils' Book ☐ A
1 *It is for someone who likes nuts and chocolate, someone who likes the story or is a Roald Dahl fan.*
2 *Probably teatime*
3 *The ingredients suggest that it would be enough for most families.*
4 *Various possible answers: using pictures, step-by-step instructions might help or separating the two recipes.*

Pupils' Book ☐ B
5

Word with a capital	Reason for a capital letter
Wonka's...	*It's the title*
Rich Tea	*It's a brand name*
Rice Crispies	*It's a brand name*

6 Ensure that children have given appropriate reasons for the use of capital letters from other extracts in the Pupils' Book.

☐ 10A Muddled instructions ⬚
The text should be in the following order, with capital letters amended and new lines for each ingredient and each step of the building process.

☐ 10B Choosing the best instructions ⬚
1 Various reasons might be given, e.g. A is better written as the structure is clearer and the layout helps the reader. The instructions are fuller. It is easier to understand.
2 A rewriting of B might look like this, ideally with new lines for each ingredient and each step of the building process.

This set of instructions for making a snowman has been muddled up.

1 Put the instructions into the right order.

2 Then put in all the capital letters that are needed.

---

what to do:

1 build a large body.

2 add on a round head.

3 put the carrot on for a nose.

4 place the hat on the head.

5 use the stones for eyes.

6 use the banana skin for a mouth.

7 you could add other extras if you wish, such as a belt, round stones for buttons, or slices of melon for ears!

making a snowman can be great fun! follow these instructions and you will soon be building the greatest snowman ever!

how to make a snowman

everybody loves snowmen. they are popular from france to russia. most children know the story of *the snowman*. it was written by raymond briggs. it is about a snowman that comes to life. who knows, if you build a snowman, it too may come alive!

what you need:

- plenty of soft snow
- 1 carrot
- 1 old hat
- 2 round, flat stones
- 1 banana skin
- warm hands

Here are two sets of instructions about favourite games that children play at breaktime in a school.

1 Decide which one is better written and why. Give at least two reasons.

2 Rewrite the worse one, improving it. Remember to make sure that the capital letters are used correctly.

A   How to play What's the time, Mr Wolf?

This is an exciting game that we play at school.
You need:
5 or more people
A space like a playground.
What to do:
One person is chosen to be Mr Wolf.
Mr Wolf walks round with everyone else following.
The children call out, 'What's the time Mr Wolf?'
Mr Wolf replies, 'one o'clock' or 'two o'clock' till he suddenly shouts 'Dinner time and I'm coming to get you'.
Then you run like mad.
The person who is captured first becomes the new Mr Wolf.
You can escape being captured if you touch the fence. It's a great game.

B   playing stick in the mud

you have to chose someone to be the chaser. we do it by saying a rhyme like one potato. Then you run around and try not to be caught. if the chaser gets you, you are frozen like a statue. that's why it is called stick in the mud because you cant move. unless someone else touches your hand. it's a laugh.

10 Capital letters

1 Sentences should always begin with a capital letter and end with a full stop, question mark or exclamation mark. For example:

The man ran down the lane!

You should make using capital letters to start a sentence a habit.

2 Capital letters are used on many other occasions. In particular, they are used for the names of:

People – *Sandy, Sam, Australians*	Days of the week – *Wednesday*
Places – *Newcastle, Africa*	Organizations – *Microsoft*
Planets – *Pluto*	Religions – *Hinduism*
Months – *January*	Shops – *Parkinson's the chemist*
	Products – *Snickers*

Remember to use a capital letter for names. It is rude if you forget!

3 Capital letters can also be used for:

Making a word seem important – *HELP!*
Signs – *STOP*   Labels – *CRAYONS*
Titles and headings – *The Silver Crown*
Initials – The *BFG*

They can be used at the start of a line in a poem:

Up early

Wood to gather
Good to hear
The sudden thwack
As axe smacks
Bare wood.

Can you think of other purposes for using capital letters?

UNIT 11 Adjectives

The purpose of this unit is to help children begin to understand the function of adjectives in sentences, and to start using adjectives effectively, so that they add extra information and colour to writing.

NLS coverage

Key objective

SL 2 To understand the function of adjectives within sentences, through:
- identifying adjectives in shared reading
- discussing and defining what they have in common, i.e. words which qualify nouns
- experimenting with deleting and substituting adjectives and noting effects on meaning
- collecting and classifying adjectives, e.g. for colours, sizes, moods
- experimenting with the impact of different adjectives through shared writing

3 To use the term adjective appropriately

Learned through:

TL Reading comprehension
3 To identify and discuss main and recurring characters, evaluate their behaviour and justify views

TL Writing composition
8 To write portraits of characters, using story text to describe behaviour and characteristics

WL 24 To explore opposites, e.g. upper/lower, rude/polite

Assessment criteria

SL By the end of this unit pupils should be able to:
- identify an adjective in a sentence
- describe the purpose of an adjective
- make choices about what adjective might be effective and give reasons for their choices

TL Writing composition
Pupils should be able to write portraits of characters, describing their behaviour and characteristics

---

Session 1

You will need OHT 11 and PCM 11A.

Shared reading

1 OHT 11: *The Unluckiest Man* is the opening of a traditional tale. Before reading this, just spend a moment tuning the children into its theme by asking what sort of unlucky things might have occurred to a main character at the start of a traditional tale.

2 Display OHT 11 and explain that some words are missed out, but that you will all read the passage through. Take initial responses from the class and then use the following questions to consider what we know about the two characters.
  - What do we know of the man's character?
  - How does he feel at the start of the story?
  - How do you think the story might end?
  - In what way do you think the man might change?
  - How does the man behave when he meets the wolf?
  - What do we know of the wolf's character?

  Encourage pupils to support their ideas with words or phrases from the text.

3 Reread the passage with two volunteers reading the parts of the man and the wolf. Discuss how the dialogue might be spoken.

Sentence level work

1 Explain that you are going to fill in the spaces in OHT 11: *The Unluckiest Man*. Gather suggestions from the class and discuss which alternative might fit the passage best. Explain that all the gap words are called adjectives and that adjectives add extra information to nouns.

If pupils are unsure about nouns, explain that nouns are labels that name objects and animals. List a few nouns round the room. Then take an animal and, as a class, list possible adjectives. For example: *shaggy, angry, silly... dog.*

This should reinforce the idea of the noun–adjective relationship, if it is necessary.

2 List on a wall chart a definition of an adjective, plus an example. Add a note to remind children why they are used. For example, one class wrote –

Adjectives describe nouns. They add extra information, telling the reader what the noun is like. Choose carefully!

3 As you are filling in the spaces on OHT 11, try adding in four or five adjectives in at least one case, e.g. *the thin, hungry, lean, grey, weary, tired, old wolf.*
   Rereading this, pupils will discover that too many adjectives sound silly.

4 Once the spaces are filled, reread the passage and underline the nouns in a different colour to the pen used to write in the adjectives. This will help pupils see the difference between the two types of words.

Independent activities

Direct pupils to PCM 11A: *Improving the adjectives.* Ask them to read the passage through or read it as a class. The writer has used the same adjective, *big*, again and again. Pupils should first underline the adjectives in one colour and the nouns in another colour. Then the task is to change the adjectives, selecting carefully for meaning and impact. Emphasize that you do not want synonyms for *big* – they must choose the most effective adjective and not always related to size!

Those who finish quickly should list the adjectives from the opening of their reading book in one column and the accompanying noun in another column. In a third column they could write another possible adjective for the noun.

Plenary

Read through PCM 11A: *Improving the adjectives,* discussing the alternative adjectives chosen by different pupils. Discuss the clues given about the main character. Focus upon the son's actions – what does each tell us about his character? Summarize by asking what the children have learned, covering the following:
- An adjective describes a noun.
- Adjectives tell the reader more about the noun, creating a picture in the reader's mind.
- It sounds silly if you use too many adjectives.
- You should not repeat the same adjective too often.

Session 2

You will need Pupils' Book Unit 11 pages 26–27 and PCM 11B.

Shared reading

Begin by recapping the work on adjectives from the previous session. Turn to *The Strange Room* in the Pupils' Book. Introduce the text as an extract from a traditional tale and read it through with the class, taking pupils' initial responses.
- What do we know about the Prince's feelings?
- What do you think Tamara is thinking about him?
- Why might they have been locked in?
- Which words has the writer used to make the meal sound disgusting?
- Which words has the writer used to make the room sound uninviting?

Sentence level work

Reread *The Strange Room* with pupils. Start a list which identifies the adjectives and nouns in the passage. (This will be continued by pupils in activity B.) Focusing upon paragraphs two and three, take a few of the adjectives and change the text by altering them. Note with pupils how by changing just these few adjectives the meal can be made to sound more appetizing or the look of the room can become more appealing.

Independent activities

Activities A and B in the Pupils' Book focus upon further altering and categorizing adjectives in the *The Strange Room.* The task is to change the adjectives more extensively in the second and third paragraphs to make the meal and room sound more pleasant.

PCM 11B: *Adjectives from traditional tales* provides a further activity for pupils who need reinforcement on adjectives or it can be used as a guided session. In this PCM, pupils are again asked to underline the adjectives, and find more interesting alternatives.

Plenary

Contrast readings of the original version of *The Strange Room* with the pupils' transformed versions. Highlight any well chosen adjectives that help to make the meal and room sound more inviting. Review the work done with PCM 11B in a similar vein.

Session 3

You will need Pupils' Book Unit 11 pages 26–27 and the Reminder Sheet.

Shared writing

Introduce the Reminder Sheet and use it to summarize the points made so far about adjectives. Explain that you are going to continue writing the story from the Pupils' Book, using adjectives effectively, keeping the same characters. Take suggestions from pupils for what might happen next and list up a few sensible incidents.

Write together

1 Once several incidents have been noted down begin to model the text. Stop at relevant nouns and consider what adjective might be used. Refer back to the Reminder Sheet so that you avoid:
   - Using too many adjectives with each noun
   - Adjectives that state what is known (wet water)
   - Repeating the same adjective
   - Using an adjective where a noun does not need it

2 Keep rereading what is being written with the children, to check the effect is the right one. Experiment with a noun and try out alternatives that might add useful layers of meaning, e.g.:
   the slim, grey wolf padded through the trees…

   Model composing a sentence before committing it to paper, to test/change ideas before writing.

3 Make sure that you maintain the characters – the bossy, bad tempered Prince must stay that way and this will influence what he says and does – unless, of course, something happens to change him.

Independent writing activity

The shared writing should lead the children directly into activity C in the Pupils' Book. Refer pupils to the Reminder Sheet to prompt their selection of adjectives. Just before the plenary ask the children to read their work and check the use of effective adjectives.

Plenary

Invite pupils to read out examples of their work. Encourage others to listen carefully and to focus on which story elements and adjectives worked well; any repetitions in the writing and how these might be overcome; any weak adjectives that might be replaced to make more impact.

As a follow up, identify well-chosen adjectives in reading and encourage their use in writing. Model this in shared writing. Collect *good* adjectives to use in pupils' spelling journals or writing journals.

Assessment

Sentence level
Notice during discussions whether children are using the term *adjective* comfortably. If not, then this is an aspect that needs revisiting in the ways discussed above in Plenary.

Writing composition
When marking, look for effective choices that illuminate the noun, especially where the choice of adjective adds an extra surprise or layer of meaning to the noun.

Model answers

Pupils' Book ⬜ A

1 The verbs suggest he is very dominant: *he strode, marched, grabbed Tamara's arm*. Also, he says *'you must do as I say'*, and *'I cannot be kept waiting'*.

2 *Strode, marched, snapped*, all suggest a military bearing and used to giving orders.

3 *He is angry and thinks 'how dare they be locked in'.*

4 *He is looking for a crystal – and possibly his father.*

5 *Yes – it is probably wrong that they were locked in.*

Pupils' Book ⬜ B

6 table: *large, broken – polished, wooden;* meal: *disgusting – nourishing;* plates: *cracked – decorated;* grapes: *rotting – plump;* puddings: *mouldy – enticing;* bread: *stale, grey – fresh, warm;* tea: *cold, yellow – hot,* milky; walls: *damp – warm;* stone: *jagged, purple – smooth, rich;* carpet: *small, worn – soft, red;* floorboards: *cold, dark – shiny, long, wooden;* paintings: *dusty – dramatic.*

7 Check pupils have listed their adjectives accurately by: Colour, Size and Look.

⬜11A   Improving the adjectives 🄿

1 Check that pupils have identified the nouns and adjectives, correctly.

⬜11B   Adjectives from traditional tales 🄿

The adjectives are: *hot, wet, sharp, big, big, slow, strong, tiny.* Interesting alternatives might be: *hot – violet; wet – frozen; sharp – blunt; big – shy; big – dainty; slow – cunning; strong – diamond; tiny – aggressive.*

Here is part of a traditional tale. The writer has been lazy and used the same adjective too many times.

1 Underline all the adjectives in one colour and the nouns in another colour.

2 Select different adjectives that improve the story and write them in.

The Big Son

Over the years the big brothers had laughed at the big son. 'You're skinny, you're stupid, you're a numbskull,' they teased.

But on this day they had a surprise. The big son picked up the big basket and made his way to the bottom of the big garden. He was determined to succeed. He stared up into the big branches of the big tree. Without hesitation he plucked a big apple. He placed it in the big basket and covered it with a big cloth.

Without a word of goodbye the big son left home. He strode across the big desert. He climbed the big mountain. He made his way down to the big river that curled like a big snake across the land. He plunged into the big water and crossed the big river. He watched the big bears scooping the big salmon up.

Then he made his way into the big forest. The big trees towered above him. He had not travelled far when he met a big woman. He stared at her big back, her big arms, her big cheeks and her big legs.

'Here,' he said. 'You may have all my food. I want nothing in return, just your blessing.'

Adjectives from traditional tales

Underline the adjectives in these sentences from different traditional tales. Change the adjectives to more interesting alternatives.

The king touched the hot flame.

The boat slipped through the wet water.

The princess pricked her thumb on the sharp needle.

The big giant roared and stamped his big feet.

The hare stared at the slow tortoise.

The wolf bit through the sword with his strong teeth.

The tiny flea bit into the Queen's skin.

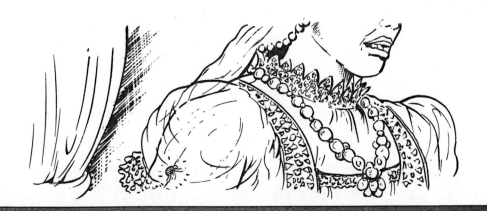

What is an adjective?

- An adjective describes a noun.
- It tells the reader more information about the noun.

How to use adjectives

- When you are writing, remember to choose adjectives carefully.
- Sometimes you do not need an adjective.

  The flames roared round the bonfire.

This sentence does not need to say: *the* hot *flames roared...*

- Try not to repeat the same adjective.

  The big shark opened its big mouth and we saw its big teeth.

- Select your adjectives carefully for more impact.

  The sleek shark opened its great mouth and we saw its sharp teeth.

- Choose adjectives that add a surprise or something new.

  The small flea tickled the large elephant.

We know that fleas are 'small' and elephants are 'large'. The adjectives add nothing new.

This sentence would be more interesting:

  The unkind flea tickled the thin elephant.

It tells us something new about both the flea and the elephant. It makes the reader wonder – why is the flea being unkind and why is the elephant thin?

1st, 2nd, or 3rd person

The purpose of this unit is to begin to establish that texts are written from different viewpoints, that the spelling of verbs alters accordingly, and that different text types usually are written in a different person. They should be able to check for consistency.

NLS coverage

Key objective

SL **10** To understand the differences between verbs in the 1st, 2nd, or 3rd person, e.g. *I/we do, you/you do, he/she/they do/does*, through:

- collecting and categorizing examples and noting the differences between the singular and plural persons
- discussing the purposes for which each can be used
- relating to different types of text, e.g. 1st person for diaries, personal letters, 2nd person for instructions, directions; 3rd person for narrative, recounts
- experimenting with transforming sentences and noting which words need to be changed

Learned through:

TL **Reading comprehension**
1 To investigate the styles and voices of traditional story language – collect examples

TL **Writing composition**
10 To write alternative sequels to traditional stories using same characters and settings

Assessment criteria

SL By the end of this unit pupils should be able to:
- identify what person a text is written in, or needs to be written in
- check for consistency of person
- adapt spellings accordingly

TL **Writing composition**
Pupils should be able to write in different text types, adapting to an appropriate style for each

Session 1

You will need OHT 12 and PCM 12A.

Shared reading

1 Introduce OHT 12: *Guess the text* and read through sentences A–J. Ask pupils to explain in what ways the sentences differ.

2 Explain that the sentences are all from different types of text. First, ask pupils to guess which type of text each sentence comes from. Then discuss how they know. Which clues give each one away?

Sentence level work

1 Point out that one difference between the sentences is whether or not they use *I, you, he*, or *she*. Examine the sentences to see whether different types of writing use 1st, 2nd, or 3rd person. Make a simple chart to show that *I* is known as 1st person, *you* as 2nd person and *he/she* as 3rd person.

2 Transform each sentence into the plural. Note how *he/she* becomes *they; you* stays as you – and *I* becomes *we*. Add this information to the chart, now showing singular and plural. Also note whether any other words in the sentences need changing.

Independent activities

Introduce PCM 12A: *From 3rd to 1st person*. Read it through. Discuss what sort of text it is and ask how pupils know this. In what person is the text written? Is it all in the same person – or does it change?

The pupils' task is to transform this story from 3rd to 1st person. When they have finished the rewriting, allow pupils time to read their version to their partners. Encourage them to use this time to make extra amendments, if the text 'doesn't sound right'.

Plenary

Discuss how narrative can be written in 1st or 3rd person. Reread the original and then listen to some examples from pupils of 1st person transformations. Which form sounds more effective and why? Ask children to spot inconsistencies or places where other words have not been altered appropriately.

Session 2

You will need Pupils' Book Unit 12 pages 28–29 and PCM 12B.

Shared reading

1 Read *Three Descriptions* in the Pupils' Book through with the children. Take their initial reactions to each. Then agree with the children on each type of writing. Discuss the clues which indicate this and encourage pupils to give evidence from the text.
   ■ In what ways do the extracts differ?
   ■ Which is your favourite extract and why?
   ■ Which extract creates the strongest picture in your mind? Describe what the picture looks like.

   These discussion points will help prepare for activity A in the Pupils' Book.

2 Discuss the audience for each extract and what the writer's purpose might be, e.g. to tell a funny story, to describe, to retell what has happened.

3 Focus on extract C. How does the writer try to make it sound exciting and dramatic? Compare the length of sentences between extract A and extract C.

Sentence level work

1 Emphasize that 1st person is used for recount/diary as in extract C – because in these forms you are writing about what happened to yourself. Extract A is in the 3rd person, and is a narrative. It is actually an extract from a tale by the storyteller, Mike Dunstan. Extract B is an oral story written down, and has a mixture of 3rd person plural and singular (they/he).

2 As a class, transform extract B into 1st person, making it into a diary entry – I/we. (*I had a budgie that my dad...*).

Independent activities

The task in activity B is to rewrite extract A in the 1st person as if it were a diary account or a letter to a friend, i.e. as if it happened to you, as if you were talking about yourself. You might wish to model this with the first line.

I had holes in the knees of my trousers, my boots were coming apart...

   Note and discuss other words that will also need changing.

   PCM 12B: *Making it the same person* offers a story text that shifts from 3rd to 1st person and back again. The pupils' task is to edit the text so that it is consistent in its use of person.

Plenary

Listen to rewrites from activity B. See if pupils can spot any inconsistencies, in sticking to the 3rd person. Contrast the differences by having one pupil read extract A in the 1st person and then another read the extract as it was originally.

   Spot-check responses to PCM 12B to ensure consistency. The majority of pupils should have chosen 3rd person for the narrative. Comment on any in the 1st person and contrast with a 3rd person version.

Session 3

You will need Pupils' Book Unit 12 pages 28–29 and the Reminder Sheet.

Shared writing

Reread extract C in the Pupils' Book. Draw pupils' attention to the person that it is written in. What advantages does this have – how does it make the writing sound?

   Discuss how the extract sounds like a diary account – some children may mention *Robinson Crusoe* as another desert island story.

   Explain that you are going to rewrite this extract in the 3rd person to make it sound more like a story.

Write together

1 Begin by reading each sentence and adapting the text accordingly. You could write the new version up on an OHT so that everyone can see the changes that are needed – or this may be done orally, depending on the confidence of the group. Less able writers will need to see the act of composition.

2 Draw children's attention to places where other words need altering to keep agreement and consistency.

3 To lead into the independent activity discuss ideas for continuing the story. Invite suggestions. On an OHT or board continue the story, sticking to 3rd person.

Independent writing activity

This rewriting of the extract will lead directly into activity C, with pupils writing the next few paragraphs in third person, describing what he or she did next. Remind them that they must ensure consistency and agreement. Distribute the Reminder Sheet to support this activity.

Plenary

Listen to several versions of the text. Ask other class members to comment on the quality of writing and ideas as well as usage of third person.

End the session by discussing whether pupils prefer stories that are written in the 1st or 3rd person. Revisit this during the term by noticing and discussing the forms in which different texts are written.

Assessment

Sentence level
Pupils should be able to identify and discuss the use of 1st, 2nd, or 3rd person in relation to different text types. They should write with grammatical agreement for common verbs, e.g. *I am, we are*, etc.

During this term include marking for agreement. In particular, draw attention to difficulties where children hop from 1st to 3rd person halfway through a text.

Writing composition
Pupils should be able to discuss and suggest what person a text might need to be written in. They should be used to check that they have not shifted tense.

Model answers

Pupils' Book ▱ **A**

1 *A – some sort of story (possible recount); B – recount or joke; C – story or diary.*

2 A – It is a description in the past tense, 3rd person. It sounds like part of a story – or possibly a recount. B – The language is informal e.g. this girl... So they got... And...and..., so... and... and. It sounds more like someone telling a joke or recounting a true event than the language of narrative. C – Present tense, the sentences sound more like a story, e.g 'when all the leaping and licking and hugging were done, I struggled to my feet' is not how you write a sentence in a recount.

3 *It sounds like someone with little money, possibly a tramp – or someone very odd!*

4 *It could be a true tale – children will volunteer all sorts of tales!*

5 *A dog – she prances, her tail circling wildly, leaping and licking.*

6 *A boat – the words are written in italics, the sea is empty, and then the writer says ' no boat'.*

7 *It sounds like a shipwreck onto a deserted island.*

Pupils' Book ▱ **B**

8 *I had holes in the knees of my trousers, my boots were coming apart, the tops from the bottoms (I'd tried to mend them by wrapping Sellotape around to hold them together), my overcoat was tied round the middle by a piece of old rope and perched on my head was a battered old felt hat.*

9 *My trousers were worn through in the seat, and my shirt was ripped. I had on an old jumper but it was torn in several places. Perched on my nose was a broken pair of glasses with only one lens. In my hand I clutched an old suitcase. I strode on, mud spattering my boots, the wind tugging through the clothes...*

▱ **12A   From 3rd to 1st person** ▱
Check that all the 3rd person aspects of the text have been changed to 1st person. For example:
Once upon a time I had a great white bear as a pet. One day I decided to walk with the bear to visit the King.

It was winter. The white bear and I walked through the forests. Snow lay on the ground and it was colder than a goblin's nose. At night I cuddled up to the bear to keep warm. I trapped small birds and rabbits to keep us both fed...

▱ **12B   Making it the same person** ▱
The rewritten 3rd person version could begin like this:
Jack looked at the hen house. It was very large. He walked into the house and peered round. It was hot and stuffy. In the darkness he could just see an enormous egg. It was not an ordinary egg. It was far too large. And it was made of gold.

Read this story carefully. Then rewrite it, changing it from 3rd to 1st person, as if writing it as a diary. Use the space below for your writing.

The Great White Bear

Once upon a time there was a man who had a great white bear as a pet. One day the man decided to walk with the bear to visit the King.

It was winter. The man and the white bear walked through the forests. Snow lay on the ground and it was colder than a goblin's nose. At night the man cuddled up to the bear to keep warm. The man trapped small birds and rabbits to keep them both fed.

One night there was a storm. It was so cold that the man began to freeze. He knew that he needed shelter. Deep in the forest he came across a cottage, so he knocked at the door.

The door opened a crack but the owner was afraid of the bear and would not let the man inside. The bear gave a growl, but still the door stayed firmly shut. How could they get in?

....
....
....
....
....
....
....
....
....
....

Read this story. The writer has muddled up 1st and 3rd person.
Change the passage so that the story is all in the same person.

Jack and the Giant Egg

Jack looked at the hen house. It was very large.
He walked into the house and peered round. It was
hot and stuffy. In the darkness he could just see an
enormous egg. It was not an ordinary egg. It was
far too large. And it was made of gold.

I stood for a moment staring at the giant egg. Just
then I heard a noise outside. An enormous chicken
blocked the doorway and it did not look too pleased
to find me inside its house. I turned and dived behind
the egg. I was not certain whether the chicken had
seen me or not.

Jack lay behind the egg. His knees were shaking
and his teeth were rattling.

He was certain that at any moment the giant
chicken would find him. Then it would peck him.
Jack wished that he had stayed at home.

12 — *Using 1st, 2nd or 3rd person*

1st person

The 1st person is used when you are writing about yourself (*I* or *we*). You use 1st person for recounts, such as news, personal letters, diaries and autobiographies.

> *When I was two years old my parents moved house.*

Some stories are written in the 1st person.

> *I stared at the path that lay ahead.*

This helps the reader feel as if they are close to the main character.

2nd person

The 2nd person is used when writing directly to a reader (*you*). It is sometimes used when writing instructions.

> *You must turn left.*

It may be used when writing explanations.

> *If you look closely you will see the screw turn. This is because...*

The 2nd person can be useful when trying to persuade people.

> *You will be certain to enjoy our new chocolate bar.*

In stories characters may use 2nd person in dialogue.

> *'You are trying to get in my way,' snarled Jake.*

3rd person

The 3rd person is used when writing about somebody else (*she*, *he* or *they*). It is often used for writing stories.

> *She ran down the steep hill.*

It can be used when writing reports.

> *He had eight wives.*

When writing ...

- Try not to start a story in the 1st person and then shift into 3rd person. In reports, keep to the 1st person.
- Make sure that the verbs agree correctly:

> *I am/We are   You are/You are   She is   or   He is/They are*

Key words for meaning

The purpose of this unit is to investigate how some words are essential to meaning – verbs and nouns – whilst others add colour – adjectives – and some help to create a fluent sentence, e.g. *the*, but are not essential to basic meaning. The unit hinges around making notes for a particular audience. It needs to be built upon by instigating note-making across the curriculum so that children are shown how to extract the key ideas, words and phrases from any text.

NLS coverage

Key objective

SL 9 To experiment with deleting words in sentences to see which are essential to meaning and which are not

Learned through:

TL Reading comprehension
17 to make clear notes through, e.g.:
- discussing the purpose of note-making and looking at simple examples
- identifying the purpose for which notes will be used
- identifying key words, phrases or sentences in reading
- exploring ways of writing ideas, messages, in shortened forms, e.g. notes, lists, headlines, telegrams, to understand that some words are more essential to meaning than others
- identifying intended audience, i.e. self or others

Assessment criteria

SL By the end of this unit, pupils should be able to:
- trim sentences down to basic meaning
- understand that verbs and nouns are essential to meaning
- understand that adjectives add colour and extra information to sentences but are not necessary to basic meaning
- begin to trim sentences to make notes by dropping inessential words and detail, given an audience and purpose

TL Writing composition
Pupils should be able to make clear notes, discussing the purpose and looking at examples

Session 1

You will need OHT 13 and PCM 13A.

Shared reading

1 Explain that in this session you will be looking at which words are needed in a sentence and which types of words can be left out.

2 Display OHT 13: *Essential words* but mask it so that only the first sentence can be seen. As you read through and finish discussion of each sentence, reveal the next until eventually the whole OHT is visible. Use these questions to prompt pupils' initial responses to each sentence.
- Does this sentence make sense?
- What type of word is missing?
- Does the sentence communicate the basic message?

Sentence level work

1 Once you reach the complete sentence on OHT 13, fill in the grid. This will confirm that:
- Nouns and verbs are shown as essential
- Adjectives add colour – or extra information – but are not essential
- *The* is useful but not necessary for basic meaning

2 The sentence under *A note for who?* is a message left for the milkman. Work with the class to trim this down to the bare essentials – what does the milkman really need to know? Turn the sentence into a note.

3 Summarize by making a simple wall chart to include the bullet pointed information above, but stressing that sentences need verbs and nouns to communicate basic meaning.

Independent activities

PCM 13A: *Keeping the basic meaning* allows pupils practice in reducing sentences to the fewest possible words without losing their main meaning. This encourages them to think again about which words are needed to retain meaning.

Plenary

Listen to pupils' suggested versions of the sentences in PCM 13A. Identify who can spot whether colour or irrelevant words have been left in.

Session 2

You will need Pupils' Book Unit 13 pages 30–31 and PCM 13B.

Shared reading

1 Before reading *Notes from Who?* in the Pupils' Book – ask the children what they notice about these texts, i.e. that they are short with not many words. Explain that these are a series of notes left for the milkman.

2 Read the notes through. Then explain to the children that the milkman works in the same village as the Jolly Postman, where characters from fairy tales and nursery rhymes live. Ask anyone to guess who left which notes. Make it like a game so they have to keep the answer to themselves. Take the *7 half pints* note and explain this relates to a fairy tale with a mirror in it and seven small people. At this stage do not let anyone give away the other notes.

3 Discuss why the notes are brief.
   ■ When leaving a note for the milkman what is essential to mention?
   ■ What does the milkman need to know?
   ■ Which two notes are briefest but have enough information so that the correct deliveries are left?

Sentence level work

Take note D that begins *No milk today*. Rewrite it with the class, leaving the bare essentials. Discuss the details which have been left out and decide why. Revisit previous work about which words are necessary to maintain the meaning.

Independent activities

Activity A in the Pupils' Book focuses on matching a well-known character to each note. In activity B pupils have to rewrite several notes, trimming them down to the key words, without omitting any crucial information for the milkman.

   PCM 13B: *Shortening the messages* contains a further three messages to be trimmed down to key meaning words. Pupils then categorize the sorts of words that have been omitted. PCM 13B is best suited to children who have begun to understand the different functions of adjectives, adverbs, verbs, and nouns so that words can be categorized successfully.

Plenary

Listen to the children's ideas about which fairy tale character wrote each note – and the clues they used to deduce this. Then hear examples of the notes trimmed back. Who managed to communicate to the milkman but with the smallest number of words?

   Review the sorts of words that can be omitted, e.g. adjectives, adverbs, some detail, words such as *please*, etc. Agree on the key words needed to maintain meaning and basic communication, e.g. verbs, nouns, and important adjectives.

Session 3

You will need Pupils' Book Unit 13 pages 30–31 and the Reminder Sheet.

Shared writing

Revisit *Notes from Who?* in the Pupils' Book and ask the class to recall what matters when writing notes. Points that could be made include.
■ You do not need all the words.
■ Nouns and verbs matter.
■ Adjectives and other words like *the* are not always needed.
■ You have to think about audience and purpose (who you are writing for and what they need to know).

Write together

1 Explain that you are going to write a telegram – a type of message or note that can be sent through the post. The problem is that you have to pay for each word. So, you only use the words that you need. Each word costs ten pounds – the challenge is to see who spends the smallest amount of money. Complete a note for Goldilocks (note listed in activity C in the Pupils' Book). Discuss who Goldilocks is writing to and what she needs to say. For example:

Mum and Dad – *Got lost in wood. Hiding in cottage. Chair and beds broken. Owner returning soon. Help!* Goldilocks.

2 Use these points to refine down briefer notes. For example:

Lost in wood. In 'Bear Cottage'. Come fetch me. Goldilocks.

Reread to check that you have spent the smallest amount of money and yet got the main points across.

Independent writing activity

The shared writing should lead directly into activity C where pupils write a telegram from another well-known fairy tale character, asking for help. Emphasize to pupils that they must not use more than 30 words.

Plenary

Listen to pupils' different versions – whose is the briefest and yet contains the main points? Invite other class members to identify unnecessary detail.

Link this introductory work on note-making to the rest of the curriculum. Carry out activities where children underline key words/ideas in texts and list them. Then show how these can be transformed into simple pieces of information. These skills are the roots of note-taking.

Assessment

Sentence level
Pupils should be able to identify key words to use in a simple message, retaining basic sense and communicating for a purpose.

They should understand that verbs are necessary to a sentence, and that adjectives add colour.

Writing composition
Pupils should be used to trimming sentences to the bare essential, so that they can make notes focused upon key facts or pieces of information.

Model answers

Pupils' Book ☐ A
1 1F, 2B, 3C, 4E, 5A, 6G, 7D, 8H

Pupils' Book ☐ B
2 C *10,001 pints gold top. Leave on top, middle or bottom step. Sentry will pay each Saturday;* E *Deliver from today, 1 best pint;* G *1/2 pint. Place ladder against bottle.* H *No milk or bread.*

☐13A Keeping the essential meaning ▣
Possible answers might include: A *Rhino charged at hunter;* B *Kite flew to highest tree;* C *Tractor rumbled down hill,* D *Tom saw toys;* E *Giant ate custard;* F *Saw snake slide towards girl.*

☐13B Shortening the messages ▣
Responses should look something like this: A *Ugly sisters – sarnies in fridge.* B *Red – Take bread and cheese to Granny's.* C *Brothers – keep wolf out.*

Shorten these sentences but keep the meaning.

A The black rhino charged at the frightened hunter.

....

....

B The red kite flew to the highest tree.

....

....

C The ancient tractor rumbled down the steep hill.

....

....

D Tom looked through the grubby window and saw the shiny toys.

....

....

E The huge giant ate the steaming bowl of custard.

....

....

F When the old door was opened they could see the green snake sliding across the floor towards the little girl.

....

....

13B Shortening the messages

1 Try to make these into the shortest possible messages.
2 Complete the chart below to show essential words and words used to give extra information in one of the passages.

A Dear Ugly Sisters,
   When you get back from the ball, I know that you will be hungry so I have left you some tasty sandwiches in the fridge.

   ....

   ....

B Dear Red Riding Hood,
   Could you please take this basket of fresh bread and soft cheeses through the dark and lonely wood to your Grandma's house?

   ....

   ....

C Dear Brothers,
   Whatever happens do not let the horrid wolf into your house as he wants to eat you up for a snack. With love from your youngest brother.

   ....

   ....

Essential words	Words that add colour	Other words
....	....	....
....	....	....
....	....	....

13 Key words for meaning

Verbs in sentences

Sentences have to have a verb or they do not make sense.

- The verb is like an engine. It gives the sentence power.
- If a sentence has no verb it cannot be understood.

  For example:
  > *The old man the green apple.*

  In this sentence you do not know what the old man did to the apple. Did he eat it, throw it, juggle with it, kick it, sell it, buy it? Without a verb you will never know.

Nouns in sentences

- Nouns are important in sentences.

  For example:
  > *The angry chased the naughty.*

  In this sentence you do not know what was angry or what it chased. Was it a teacher chasing a child, or a lion chasing a cub? Without a noun you will never know.

- Adjectives, like *angry* and *naughty* add colour to nouns.

  They tell the reader what the noun looked like. They give us more information. You do not need them for the sentence to make sense.

  For example:
  > *The angry dog chased the naughty boy.*

  This sentence still makes sense if you take out the adjectives.
  > *The dog chased the boy.*

- When you are writing notes think about whom you are writing for and exactly what they need to know. Thinking carefully about key nouns and verbs will help you write notes most effectively.

14 *Commas*

The purpose of this unit is to draw children's attention to commas within reading and to show how they help readers to pause. Commas are returned to later in the framework. The emphasis is noticing commas in reading. In this instance the focus is on the dramatic reading of poetry.

NLS coverage

Key objective

SL 6 To note where commas occur in reading and to discuss their functions in helping the reader

7 To use the term *comma* appropriately in relation to reading

Learned through:

TL **Reading comprehension**

4 To choose and prepare poems for performance, identifying appropriate expression, tone, volume and use of voices and other sounds

5 Rehearse and improve performance, taking note of punctuation

TL **Writing composition**

11 To write new or extended verses for performance based on models of 'performance' and oral poetry reading, e.g. rhythms, repetition

Assessment criteria

SL By the end of this unit pupils should be able to:
- use the term comma when discussing reading
- take notice of commas when reading
- discuss how commas help the reader

TL **Writing composition**
Pupils should be able to write new or extended verses for a poem for performance

Session 1

You will need OHT 14 and PCM 14A.

Shared reading

1 Display OHT 14: *I am Wunk*. Explain that this is a poem by an American writer, Jack Prelutsky. Read the text through with pupils several times. You may wish to ignore the pauses for the commas – or at least, refrain from emphasizing them.

2 Take pupils' initial responses to *I am Wunk*:
- Do you like the poem?
- What do you like about it?
- How do you think the poet felt when he wrote this?
- What special effect has the poet used in the first two lines?
- In the first verse what three things does the wizard change the reader into?

- Name the three things that the wizard does with the crystal sphere.
- Name the two things the magic hat does.

Sentence level work

1 Begin to focus on the commas in the poem. Take the first verse and underline the commas. Reread the poem emphasizing the pauses. Contrast this with a reading where you rush over the commas. Which reading sounds more effective? Explain that commas are the poet's directions to the reader to pause.

2 Take the first two lines and look at how the commas isolate an extra 'bit of information'. Use the pattern as a basis for inventing similar sentences. You could do this simply by listing other alliterative names for a wizard, goblin, dwarf, hobbit, elf, dragon, sprite, e.g. *William, Gerald, Donald, Harry, Elspeth, Dirk, Sam*, etc. Then use the names to create new sentences. For example:
I am Gerald, a gorgeous goblin,
And I grab a golden glass.

The alliteration may be abandoned if it is too hard or it becomes a straight-jacket. You could move away from mythical peoples to include animals, e.g. *I am Simon, a sulky seal,/and I swim the ocean seas.*

3 When you have modelled several examples, pupils should have sufficient understanding to write their own sentences. Before doing this, reread the model sentences, paying attention to the dramatic pause that each comma requires.

Independent activities

1 Ask pupils to write poetry sentences of their own either about people, animals, or mythical creatures. They should directly imitate the sentence structure that has been modelled, and be prepared to read their ideas aloud.

2 PCM 14A ask pupils to read *I am Wunk* and in one colour mark all the commas. In another colour they mark the full stops. This shows where to pause, and where to stop. Pairs or groups then prepare a reading.

Plenary

End this session by hearing some readings of the original poem as well as some of the pupils' own sentences. The emphasis should be upon:

- Speaking loudly and clearly enough to be heard
- Speaking with expression
- Varying the pace and volume for effect
- Paying attention to commas and full stops
- If working in pairs or groups, making effective use of different voices

Session 2

You will need Pupils' Book Unit 14 pages 32–33 and PCM 14B.

Shared reading

1 Before reading *My Dad, Your Dad* in the Pupils' Book, quickly revisit what pupils have learned about commas from Session 1. Commas are useful because they tell the reader when to pause in a sentence, especially when reading aloud.

2 Just before reading the poem, ask pupils what looks odd about it, i.e. that some verses are in italic. Explain that you will all read the poem together and then discuss why the poet has used italics.

3 After the first reading, take suggestions as to why some verses are in italic. Some pupils will have realized that it is a conversation poem and that the

italics show a second person is speaking. Reread the poem using two halves of the class for the different voices. You could read it again with all girls/all boys to gain a greater contrast.

4 Explore with pupils the following questions.
- Are the children being rude?
- Are the children exaggerating?
- What sort of things do you boast about?
- What sort of effect is the poet trying to create?
- Who do you think would enjoy reading the poem?

Sentence level work

Now look carefully at the punctuation. Notice the commas in the first two lines. Reread these to the children without pauses and with pauses. Listen to the effect that the pausing gives, especially to emphasize the word *Yes*. Carry out the same activity with the first chorus. Practise reading this with the class, pausing on the commas.

Independent activities

Activity B in the Pupils' Book is to prepare a paired reading of the poem, taking special notice of the pauses that the commas suggest. PCM 14B is a photocopiable version of *My Dad, Your Dad* which can be used as part of homework. This will allow pupils to rehearse their reading, learn their parts, and prepare for a full duologue by the end of the unit.

Plenary

First take feedback on different answers to activity A. This can be followed by some paired readings. Encourage listeners to evaluate these and repeat examples where good expression is used. Make a class list headed: *To read a poem aloud you need to...* Include ideas such as: Read clearly, Do not read too quickly, Make sure everyone can hear, Say the words clearly so the audience can understand, Vary the volume, Vary the pace, Read with expression, Pause at the commas and stop at the full stops.

Session 3

You will need Pupils' Book Unit 14 pages 32–33 and the Reminder Sheet.

Shared reading

1 Reread Kit Wright's poem in the Pupils' Book. Explain that you are going to write a new version of the poem together. This time the two Dads/Mums are discussing their children (sons/daughters). Draw

the pupils' attention to the need for using italics to distinguish who is speaking and remind them about the use of commas to indicate a pause within sentences. Distribute the Reminder Sheet for support in this. (Some pupils will also know that commas are used when writing a list.)

Write together

1 Focus upon the sentence structure within the first verse of the original and use this as a basis to invent a parody. For example:

My son's... than your son,
Yes, my son's... than yours:
If he gets any...
He...

Do not worry about securing a rhyme. Just imitate the basic structure. It may be useful to begin by brainstorming what the son or daughter might be – thinner, fatter, quicker, slower, etc.

2 Then begin to fill the structure in. For example:

My son's thinner than your son,
Yes, my son's thinner than yours:
If he gets any thinner... ... ...

Indeed the first three lines are simply a matter of fitting in the selected abuse! The thinking has to begin with the final line:

He might slip through the floorboards.

To secure the last line, pupils just have to think about what awful thing might befall someone who gets very thin, is very fat, is too quick or terribly slow.

3 Create at least two verses as a class and ensure that the basic verse structure is clear for everyone to see.

Independent writing activity

Following on from the shared writing, pupils write their own verses, taking care to use the established structure.

They can then prepare a reading of their work and should be allowed five minutes working in pairs to practise reading the verses to each other. Use the Reminder Sheet as a prompt for their reading aloud – including drawing their attention to taking notice of punctuation.

Plenary

Listen to some of the children's verses. Use the Reminder Sheet to help children evaluate readings and invite constructive comment from listeners.

Assessment

Sentence level
Pupils should be able to use the term comma appropriately.
They should be able to identify and discuss the function of a comma in reading as a way of pausing or isolating extra information or detail in a sentence.

Writing composition
Pupils should be able to write simple extensions to poems where the form is clear and straightforward.

Model answers

Pupils' Book ☐ **A**

1 Various possible answers: e.g. *they are friends mucking about; they are competitive; they want their Dad to be the silliest; it's an amusing competition.*

2 *He is so fat that if he eats anymore he won't fit in the house.*

3 *He is so dim that he has to look at his watch to check if it is night or day.*

4 *He only has two, grey hairs left.*

5 *They don't mind each other; they quite like each other.*

6 *The second and fourth lines rhyme.*

7 *We know that the children think that the Dads might not think much of them, so answers might include:* they are silly, daft, naughty, crazy, irritating, etc.

Pupils' Book ☐ **B**

8 Draw pupils' attention to reading with expression and clarity as well as using the punctuation to help the reading.

☐ **14A   Taking note of the pauses** 🄿
Check that all commas and full stops have been marked on the PCM.

Read *I am Wunk* again. In one colour, mark all the commas.
In another colour, mark the full stops This now shows where to
pause, and where to stop. It will help you to prepare a reading of the
poem to share with the class.

I am Wunk

I am Wunk, a wacky wizard,
and I wield a willow wand.
I wave it once, and there you swim,
a minnow in a pond.
I wave it twice, and there you sit,
a lizard on a log.
I wave it thrice, and there you fly,
a fly before a frog.

I am Wunk, a wily wizard,
and I hold a crystal sphere.
I spin it with my fingers,
you've a carrot in your ear.
I roll it on the table,
you've an anvil on your head.
I place it on your pillow,
you've a lion on your bed.

I am Wunk, the wondrous wizard,
and I wear a woollen hat.
I take it off and fold it,
you are smaller than a cat.
I put it in my pocket,
you are smaller than a mouse.
Do be quick, your doorbell's ringing...
I am Wunk outside your house.

Jack Prelutsky

'I am Wunk', from *Something Big Has Been Here* (published in the UK by Heinemann Young
Books, a division of Egmont Children's Books Ltd, London, 1990), copyright © Jack Prelutsky
1989, reprinted by permission of the publishers

Use this page to make notes for your reading of the poem.

My Dad, Your Dad

My dad's fatter than your dad,
Yes, my dad's fatter than yours:
If he eats any more he won't fit in the house,
He'll have to live out of doors.

Yes, but my dad's balder than your dad,
My dad's balder, OK,
He's only got two hairs left on his head
And both are turning grey.

Ah, but my dad's thicker than your dad,
My dad's thicker, all right.
He has to look at his watch to see
If it's noon or the middle of the night.

Yes, but my dad's more boring than your dad.
If he ever starts counting sheep
When he can't get to sleep at night, he finds
It's the sheep that go to sleep.

But my dad doesn't mind your dad.
Mine quite likes yours too.
I suppose they don't always think much of US!
That's true, I suppose, that's true.

Kit Wright

'My Dad, Your Dad,' by Kit Wright from *Rabbiting On, and Other Poems* (Fontana Young Lions, 1978), reprinted by permission of the author

14 Commas

Commas in sentences

1 Commas are used for items in a list. For example:

> *I bought a cat, a dog, a rat and a mouse.*

2 Commas are used in poetry to indicate a pause.

> *My Dad's fatter than your Dad,*
> *Yes, my Dad's fatter alright.*

3 Commas are used to add in extra information to a sentence.

> *I am Wunk, the wily wizard, and I wield my willow wand.*
>
> In the above sentence the phrase *the wily wizard* is an extra piece of information dropped into the sentence by the writer.

Performing poetry

When you are reading poems aloud you must remember to:

- Speak the words clearly so the audience can understand them.
- Speak loudly enough to be heard.
- Vary the volume – sometimes loud, sometimes softer for effect.
- Read with expression.
- Vary the pace – sometimes fast, sometimes slow.
- Use different voices for effect.
- Pay attention to the punctuation: stop at full stops; pause at commas; exclaim at exclamation marks; raise tone of voice at question marks.

TERM 3

UNIT 15 *Grammatical agreement*

The purpose of this unit is to revise and help pupils to articulate the ways in which knowledge of sentence grammar can support them in reading, in conjunction with other reading skills. Pupils will also begin to learn about grammatical agreement.

NLS coverage

Key objective

[SL] **1** To use awareness of grammar to decipher new or unfamiliar words; to use this in conjunction with other strategies when reading
3 To ensure grammatical agreement in speech and writing of pronouns and verbs, e.g. *I am, we are,* in standard English

Learned through:

[TL] **Reading comprehension**
2 To refer to significant aspects of the text, e.g. opening, build-up, atmosphere, and to know language is used to create these
4 To consider credibility of events, e.g. by selecting some real life adventures and comparing them with fiction

[TL] **Writing composition**
11 To write openings to stories or chapters linked to or arising from reading; to focus on language to create effects

[WL] **12** To collect new words from reading; create ways of categorizing and logging them; infer the meaning of unknown words from context

Assessment criteria

[SL] By the end of this unit, pupils should be able to:
- articulate how awareness of grammar can help them in tackling new or unfamiliar words in texts
- edit text to check for agreement of pronouns and verbs

[WL] Pupils should be able to write an opening for a mystery or adventure story

Session 1

You will need OHT 15 and PCM 15A.

Shared reading

1 Begin by reviewing the openings of some stories that the class has read. Which openings do children remember best? Why is this?

Ask pupils to look again at how these stories begin. Some stories begin with description, some with action, some with dialogue. Are there any other possibilities?

2 Explain that you are going to read the beginning of a story. Display and read OHT 15: *Did You Hear That?* Ask pupils to work in pairs to discuss what sort of story this might be. They should find two clues to prove this, and share them with the rest of the class. Gather these clues together. Examine which are the most obvious; does everyone agree with all the clues? Are any of them ambiguous?

3 Look again at the story opening. Ask pupils:
- Which type of opening has the writer chosen?
- Is it effective? Why?

Sentence level work

1 Ask pupils to identify any words in OHT 15: *Did You Hear That?* which they think are unusual. Revise ways of using grammar to read these words as part of a reminder to pupils of the four main cueing systems in reading:
- Context – what sort of a text is this? Can we use pictures to help us, or knowledge about the subject?
- Grammar – what sort of word might come next? Can we use what we know about sentences to help us read the word?

- Sight vocabulary – if we don't know the word, then we can use this to look for parts of words we know in the new word.
- Phonics – what do we know about letters, or other words which could help us to read the word?

2 Explain to pupils that readers can use these skills in conjunction with each other, for example predicting from context and grammar, and then using word level skills to check these predictions.

Demonstrate this by writing up some sentences:
Both girls stood still, listening intently.
Which word here is difficult?

Ask if any of the pupils know what *intently* means. If not, cover up the word and ask children for suggestions as to what the word might be. They may suggest: *carefully*, *quietly*, or *hard*. A number of suggestions will end in *-ly*, as the sentence grammar suggests an adverb. Pupils may not know this term, but they should understand that the word tells more about the way in which the girls listened.

Now look at the ways in which the word can be built up, by looking at words within words. And finally put all the strategies together.

Ask pupils if they can now guess the meaning of the word *intently*. Referring to a thesaurus or dictionary will help them to compare definitions.

Independent activities

PCM 15A: *The story continues* is a cloze procedure exercise that follows the story begun in OHT 15. The task is to select words which fit grammatically.

Plenary

Take feedback on pupils' work on PCM 15A, paying attention to particularly effective answers which enhance the story and to any problem areas.

Summarize with pupils what they have learnt about how grammar can help reading and about grammatical agreement in this session.

Session 2

You will need OHT 15, Pupils' Book Unit 15 pages 34–35 and PCM 15B.

Shared reading

Explain that you will be reading an opening to another story. Ask pupils to think about what sort of story this is going to be as you read *The Vanishment of Thomas Tull* from the Pupils' Book.

1 Talk about this as an opening to a story. Invite pupils' predictions about what is going to happen in the rest of the story.

2 Compare this with the opening they read in OHT 15 in the last session.
- This story doesn't open with dialogue. What sort of opening is it?
- Do you think it works well?
- Does it make you want to read more?

Sentence level work

Revise idea of grammatical agreement. Explain that when we write, we may not know the person who is going to read what we have written. It is important, therefore, that we use the rules of English grammar more carefully than we do when talking to friends.

If you are writing about more than one thing, you should make sure that the verbs are plural.

Explain that you are going to write up three sentences, of which two are grammatically accurate. They will find these groupings easier than judging sentences in isolation. For example:

The cars are parked	is right
The car is parked	is right, but
The cars is parked	is wrong.

I was going home	is right, and
We were going home	is right, but
We was going home	is wrong.

Encourage children to identify any difficulties and to express these in their own language.

Independent activities

Activity A in the Pupils' Book encourages children to look closely at the meaning of the extract from *The Vanishment of Thomas Tull*.

Activity B asks children to look more closely at agreement of pronouns and verbs.

PCM 15B: *Checking the agreement* provides another story text where the pupils' task is to ensure consistent agreement.

Plenary

Listen to pupils' responses to PCM 15B and discuss any instances where they found it hard to make the correct agreement.

Conclude the session by reviewing the way in which grammar can help when reading. List the different strategies available to readers, and how grammatical awareness can be used alongside phonic strategies, context and picture cues, and recognition of letter strings to aid pupils' reading.

Session 3

You will need Pupils' Book Unit 15 pages 34–35 and the Reminder Sheet.

Shared writing

Explain that you are going to write the opening of a story which you will be working on for some time. It will be an adventure or mystery story. Explore the plot possibilities. On this occasion you will just write the opening, but there are some decisions to be made before you start.

Have a clear idea where the story is going. Specify the number of characters – three or four – and a rough idea of the plot structure. For example: three children go on a trip to a castle, miss the bus home and get stuck overnight, think they hear a ghost but eventually find it was a stray cat, and are found by a search party.

Write together

1 Introduce the Reminder Sheet, drawing pupils' attention to the different options for the opening. Experiment with each one. Encourage pupils to discuss these and adopt their preferred opening. Reinforce basic punctuation and grammatical agreement as you write.

2 Discuss possibilities for moving through the opening scene – what is going to happen, who will do what? Draw up a simple four-frame storyboard for the scene. Pupils can refer to this as they write.

Independent writing activity

Following on from the shared writing, pupils continue writing the story, following the outline in the storyboard. Once they have completed the first scene as part of activity C, they should exchange openings with a friend. Each child should give feedback to their partner on what they like about their opening and anything that could be done to improve it.

Plenary

Children read out sentences from their story openings with which they are particularly pleased and ask others to confirm that the subjects and verbs agree in each case.

Assessment

Sentence level
In guided reading, comment on the extent to which pupils use grammatical cues spontaneously. When marking writing, draw attention to agreement between pronouns and verbs. Encourage pupils to correct them themselves.

Writing composition
Comment on the extent to which pupils have used language for specific effect. Ask them to identify the effects for themselves.

Model answers

Pupils' Book ☐ A
1 *Narrative/story*
2 *No*
3 *Could: stop growing*
  Could not: shrinking
4 *He probably doesn't like it. He might feel embarrassed and silly. He wouldn't want to be different from all his friends.*

Pupils' Book ☐ B
5 *Thomas Tull was seven when he stopped growing.*
  Thomas Tull's parents were very worried about him.
  If I was Thomas Tull's parent, I would take him to see the doctor.

☐ 15A   The story continues ⚏
This PCM requires pupils to think about which speech verbs and adverbs they will employ as well as focusing on agreement. Comment on the aptness of their choices as well as their accuracy in making agreement.

☐ 15B   Checking the agreement ⚏
Sam was the tallest boy in <u>his</u> class. He <u>was</u> only eight years old, but he looked like a ten <u>year-old</u>. Sam <u>hated</u> being tall. He wanted to be shorter, like <u>his</u> best friend Ben.

Ben and Sam went everywhere together. <u>They</u> played together, sat together in school and walked home together. People <u>laughed</u> at them because they <u>looked</u> so different, but nothing could split <u>them</u> up.

One day at the start of the school holidays, Sam and Ben saw a poster for a circus in a shop window. Something else they could <u>do</u> together – or so Sam thought at first.

15A *The story continues*

1 The next part of the story has not been finished properly. The writer needs your help to choose words that would fit in the gaps. Can you help?

2 Look at the rest of the writing. Are there any other parts of the story you could change to make it better?

Jenny sat down in the corner. Anna picked up the

teddy bear she had been _____ for.

'Look!' she _____

'Sssssshhh!' _____ Jenny _____.

The noises had stopped. Anna went to sit by Jenny.

Now they were _____ scared. They held hands.

'I know,' _____ Jenny, 'do you think we could

'phone the police?'

Before _____ could move, there was a loud

crash. Someone had tripped over Jenny's bag.

'Oh, no!' said a voice. It was a voice _____ both

_____.

'Dad!' _____ _____ _____.

_____, they opened the door, and _____

down the stairs.

15ʙ Checking the agreement

This story opening has not been checked. Look for the mistakes and correct them.

The Tallest Boy

Sam was the tallest boy in him class. He were only eight years old, but he looked like a ten year-old. Sam hates being tall. He wanted to be shorter, like her best friend Ben.

Ben and Sam went everywhere together. Them played together, sat together in school and walked home together. People laughing at them because they look so different, but nothing could split they up.

One day at the start of the school holidays, Sam and Ben saw a poster for a circus in a shop window. Something else they could does together – or so Sam thought at first.

Grammatical agreement

- In writing, it is important to use words that agree with each other. You don't always do this when talking to people you know. When you write, you have to be more careful.

- If you are writing about more than one thing, you should make sure that the verb is plural.

The cars are parked.	is right
The car is parked.	is right, but
The cars is parked.	is wrong.
I was going home.	is right, and
We were going home.	is right, but
We was going home.	is wrong.

Writing story openings

- Writers choose different ways to open stories, but they all want readers to carry on reading. They may start a story with:
  - dialogue,
  - a startling or intriguing statement,
  - a character description, or
  - a description of the setting.

The purpose of this unit is to encourage pupils to extend sentences, using connectives other than simple ones. Pupils will also begin more extended pieces of story writing.

NLS coverage

Key objective

SL 5 To understand how sentences can be joined in more complex ways through using a widening range of conjunctions in addition to *and* and *then*
6 To investigate through reading and writing how words and phrases can signal time sequences, e.g. *first, then, after, meanwhile, from, where*

Learned through:

TL Reading comprehension
1 To retell main points of a story in sequence; to compare stories; to evaluate stories and justify their preferences
2 To refer to significant aspects of the text, e.g. opening, build-up, atmosphere, and to know that language is used to create these
5 To discuss characters' feelings, behaviour and relationships, referring to the text and making judgements

TL Writing composition
10 To plot a sequence of episodes modelled on a known story, as a plan for writing

11 To write openings to stories or chapters linked to or arising from reading; to focus on language and effects, e.g. building tension, suspense, creating moods, setting scenes
13 To write more extended stories based on a plan of incidents and set out in simple chapters

Assessment criteria

SL By the end of this unit, pupils should be able to:
■ join sentences in different ways in speech and writing
■ identify and use in writing a range of Temporal Connectives

TL Writing composition
Pupils should be able to plan and write a longer story

Session 1

You will need OHT 16 and PCM 16A.

Shared reading

1 Explain to pupils that you are going to read the middle of a story about two girls who are hiding in their playroom from burglars. Working in pairs, ask pupils to discuss how they would react in the same situation. Each pair should write down two words or phrases to describe the way they think the girls may be feeling.
2 Display and read OHT 16: *Not a Single Sound*. Ask pupils to look back at their notes and invite them to say whether they feel they were close in their

predictions. Look at the evidence in the text and use these questions to further the discussion.
■ What is the best word to describe the girls' feelings (e.g. scared, frightened, terrified)? What evidence is there in the text?
■ How do Anna and Jenny behave towards each other?
■ Is this the end of the story?

Sentence level work

1 Begin by drawing pupils' attention to different lengths of sentence in OHT 16. Some are short, some are long. Ask pupils to find the shortest sentence. (Check that they all have the same idea of sentence length, i.e. they are counting number of words, not letters!)
Gradually, Jenny relaxed.

Look at the sentence in some detail. First of all, consider the use of the word gradually. What does this word tell pupils about how Jenny relaxed? How long do they think it might have taken? Remind them that it happened between Anna phoning the police and the girls hearing the siren – probably a few minutes.

This is a very short sentence. How much information does this sentence provide?

2 Now, look at some of the longer sentences. Ask pupils to look for the longest. Write it up on a board. *Jenny felt close to tears; she thought the men might be able to hear her heart thumping in her chest.*

Explore how much information this sentence offers? It tells us how Jenny feels, what she is thinking, and how her heart is beating. Is there anything else? Can the sentence be split up into smaller sentences? Ask pupils to work on this and arrive at a model similar to this one.

Jenny felt close to tears. Her heart was thumping in her chest. She thought the men might be able to hear it.

Compare the two versions. In the original, the first clause is linked to the rest of the sentence by a semi-colon. What does this linking achieve? Ask children why Jenny feels tearful – perhaps it was because she was frightened the men could hear her heart. Linking the sentences in this way makes this clearer.

3 Summarize the main points of this session: writers put sentences together in ways which tell readers about the order in which things happened, and show how one thing happened because of another. They do this using connecting words and phrases and punctuation.

Independent activities

PCM 16A: *Connecting sentences* allows pupils the opportunity to practise joining sentences. It offers very clear models to support them in this task.

Plenary

Listen to pupils' suggested versions of the sentences in PCM 16A and talk about the connecting words which are best at making the meaning clear.

Session 2

You will need Pupils' Book Unit 16 pages 36–37 and PCM 16B.

Shared reading

1 Explain that in the next session you will be writing the next part of Jenny and Anna's story together. You are going to prepare for this by reading an extract from another mystery story. This story is set in an old castle, during a school visit. The main character, William, is on his own, doing some drawing.

2 Read *William and the Ghost* in the Pupils' Book. Ask pupils how they think William feels during these events. Take each paragraph in turn.
- Unusual things happen in the first paragraph – what are they? How would they have felt?
- What do you think of William's reaction to the dog in the second and third paragraphs? It must look very friendly!
- How does the writer tell readers that there is something unusual about the dog?
- Find the words and phrases in the extract that suggest spookiness – (e.g. dark, damp, the fact that William feels cold, and that the suit of armour has moved since he drew it.)

Sentence level work

1 Examine the way in which the writer has connected ideas and events. Ask pupils to identify connecting words and phrases, e.g. *suddenly, then, and, as.*

2 Remind them that they can use these connectives in their own stories. Working in threes, gets pupils to think of five more connectives like these. Go around to each group, building up a list to which children can refer later when writing.

3 Now select some sentences which may be useful in the shared writing session. Highlight some such as these and discuss them:
As William watched, a small door began to open at the back of the fire-place.
The dog barked, looked at William, and walked to the door in the fire-place.
The little dog looked back to make sure that William was following, and went through the door.

Ask the class to decide which three would be most useful. Write them onto a chart/OHT for reference.

Independent activities

Activity B in the Pupils' Book asks pupils to select connectives to link some of the shorter sentences in *William and the Ghost.*

PCM 16B: *Putting sentences back together* is a simpler matching activity for pupils who may need a stepping stone to activity B in the Pupils' Book.

Plenary

Ask pupils to share their responses to activity B and get class members to comment on the successful linking of shorter sentences. Consider how connectives help to bring out the full meaning in the longer sentences.

Session 3

You will need Pupils' Book Unit 16 pages 36–37 and the Reminder Sheet.

Shared writing

1 Explain that you are going to write the next part of Jenny and Anna's story.

   Begin by looking at the structure of OHT 16 that you read together in Session 1.

   Ask pupils to identify stages in the extract. Then work with them, on a chart like this, to give each stage a tension rating.

Story stage	Tension rating (1–5)
Girls hiding in room Phone rings Men leave Girls hear siren	

2 Now ask, if this is not the end of the story, what has to happen? The tension has to increase! Look at using a similar pattern of increasing and then decreasing tension for the final episode.

   Consider what the events might be, reviewing the previous events in the story. Then outline these in a chart like the one below.

Write together

Once pupils are happy with the structure of the sequence, begin writing. Draw their attention to the style of the original piece, including variation in sentence length. Model use of punctuation, particularly commas within sentences.

Independent writing activities

The shared writing should lead directly into pupils planning and writing a continuation of *William and the Ghost* for activity C in the Pupils' Book. Encourage them to plan out the events and to think carefully about using sentences of varying lengths to maintain the reader's interest and to create tension and supense.

Distribute the Reminder Sheet which covers suggested sentence structures upon which children can draw.

As an alternative pupils could continue writing the Anna and Jenny story and make up their own exciting ending.

Plenary

Children share the endings of their stories, and explain which sentences they found most useful as reminders of how to write extended sentences that convey meaning clearly. They may also like to identify which connectives they found most effective.

Assessment

Sentence level
In responding to writing, comment on the range of sentence types. In guided sessions, encourage pupils to look for opportunities for combining sentences. Comment on the range of temporal connectives pupils have used.

Writing composition
Comment upon the structure of the story – did pupils follow their plan? Are they happy with the final product?

Model answers

Pupils' Book A

1 *The suit of armour*
2 *He might be doing it for school.*
3 *A secret passage*
4 *Followed it for an adventure / stayed put – frightened / gone to find friends – get help*

Pupils' Book B

5 *He looked at his drawing, and then at the armour.*
   He began to feel rather strange, because the arm of the suit of armour had moved.
   The dog wagged its tail, and William followed it through the door.

16A Connecting sentences

There are many possibilities for joining these sentences. Models have been included to help pupils. Here are some examples:
Suddenly the door was opened by the boys coming in.
When one girl giggled, the sad-looking blonde one sniffed.
Philip saw the dog stand up, then start running.
When he saw the baby was awake, John switched off the TV.

16B Putting sentences back together

A *The boy stood up, opened his bag and put the books in it.*
B *As David watched, a bird flew down from a tree.*
C *Susan ran up the stairs and into her bedroom.*
D *Andrew pushed the door open and found himself in a video shop.*

Connecting sentences

Look at the sentences in A–D and the longer sentences that have been made from them. Then join the sentences below them to make a similar longer sentence. These should make the meaning clearer.

A The silence was broken. The telephone rang.
Suddenly the silence was broken by the telephone ringing.

The door was opened. The boys came in.

....

B The younger one spoke. He sounded scared.
When the younger man spoke he sounded scared.

One of the girls giggled. The blonde one sniffed. She looked sad.

....

C Jenny and Anna heard the door open. The door closed.
Jenny and Anna heard the door open, and then close.

Philip saw the dog stand up. The dog started running.

....

D The coast was clear. Anna called the police.
As soon as she was sure the coast was clear, Anna called the police.

The baby was awake. John switched off the television.

....

Sentences A–D have been cut in half and mixed up. See if you can join them back together again.

Beginning	End
A The boy stood up, opened his bag	and found himself in a video shop.
B As David watched	and into her bedroom.
C Susan ran up the stairs	and put the books in it.
D Andrew pushed the door open	a bird flew down from the tree.

A

....

....

B

....

....

C

....

....

D

....

....

Using different types of sentence

When you are writing a story, try to use different types of sentences. This helps to keep the reader interested, and to make links between events. Here are some examples of sentences to give you ideas.

> *As William watched, a small door began to open at the back of the fire-place.*
>
> *The dog barked, looked at William, and walked to the door in the fire-place.*
>
> *William followed it through the door and found himself in a dark passage.*
>
> *The little dog looked back to make sure that William was following, and went through the door.*
>
> Adapted from *William and the Ghost* (Oxford Reading Tree 1988), reprinted by permission of Oxford University Press

Connecting words

You can also use words to connect parts of your story, for example:

suddenly	*when*	*then*	*next*	*later*
and	*then*	*soon*	*afterwards*	

UNIT 17 *Personal pronouns*

The purpose of this unit is to introduce children to pronouns; they will look at their function in language through the fiction of Jacqueline Wilson.

NLS coverage

Key objective

SL 2 To identify pronouns and understand their functions in sentences through:
- noticing in speech and reading how they stand in place of nouns
- substituting pronouns for common and proper nouns in own writing

Learned through:

TL **Reading comprehension**

4 To consider credibility of events in stories, e.g. ... real life adventures and ... fiction

8 To compare and contrast works by the same author

9 To discuss preferences for authors and reasons for them

TL **Writing composition**

14 To write book reviews for a specified audience, based on plot, characters, and language

Assessment criteria

SL By the end of this unit, pupils should be able to:
- identify pronouns in texts
- use pronouns appropriately in their own writing

TL **Writing composition**

Pupils should be able to write a review for a specific audience

Session 1

You will need OHT 17 and PCM 17A.

Shared reading

1 Explain to the class that you are going to look at the work of a popular writer called Jacqueline Wilson. If any pupils have read her books invite them to say whether the book was funny, serious, or sad and what they liked or disliked about it.

2 Before reading OHT 17: *The Dinosaur's Packed Lunch*, explain that Dinah is on a trip with her class but she has no packed lunch. Display the OHT and read it through with the class, taking their initial responses.
- How does Dinah feel at the beginning / the end?
- Why is Dinah described as feeling empty?
- Which events are realistic and which are not?
- Would you like to read more of it? Why?

Sentence level work

Explain that you are going to look at pronouns – a group of words that speakers and writers use instead of nouns. What would happen if they did not, e.g.: *Sometimes Judy shared Judy's packed lunch with Dinah*, instead of *Sometimes*

Judy shared her packed lunch with Dinah.

Ask children to comment upon the two sentences. Which seems better and why? Experiment with some others, replacing pronouns with proper nouns.

Independent activities

PCM 17A: *Putting in the pronouns* is based on the beginning of *The Dinosaur's Packed Lunch* and offers pupils practice in working with pronouns.

Plenary

Invite one pupil to read the correct version of the extract from PCM 17A; the class mark their own work. Discuss the results and the effect of using pronouns.

Session 2

You will need Pupils' Book Unit 17 pages 38–39 and PCM 17B.

Shared reading

1 Introduce the extract from *The Suitcase Kid* in the Pupils' Book. Do pupils know Wilson's writing?

2 Read the extract through with the class and take their initial responses, especially to the narrator. Explain this term, if they do not already know it.
- Is the narrator male or female?
- How old is the narrator?
- How does s/he feel about the other characters?

3 Ask children what they think about this extract. Which book would they rather read – *The Dinosaur's Packed Lunch* or *The Suitcase Kid?* – and why?

Sentence level work

1 Direct pupils to one of the differences between the two texts: one is in the 3rd and one in the 1st person. Ask them which is which and how they know this. The biggest clues are the pronouns.

2 Look for pronouns in *The Suitcase Kid*. Discuss how often Wilson uses proper nouns and pronouns; how she signposts for the reader who is doing what, by not using pronouns all the time.

Independent activities

PCM 17B: *Highlighting pronouns* allows pupils to practise tracking characters through the extract from *The Dinosaur's Packed Lunch*. The task is to highlight all the pronouns and instances of characters' names in distinct colours to show their actions in the story. This can be used as an extension to the sentence level work. Activity B in the Pupils' Book invites children to transform sentences from the 1st to the 3rd person.

Plenary

Ask individual pupils to read out their sentences from activity B and discuss the effect of tracking characters through pronouns with those who completed PCM 17B.

Session 3

You will need Pupils' Book Unit 17 pages 38–39 and the Reminder Sheet.

Shared writing

Use the Reminder Sheet to summarize. Then briefly revisit the extract from *The Suitcase Kid*. Explain that you are going to begin rewriting the text as Katie.

Write together

Model the first part of Katie's version of events, highlighting the use of 1st person pronouns as you write. Encourage pupils to think about Katie's character and how their writing should reflect this.

Independent writing activity

The shared writing should lead to activity C in the Pupils' Book, with pupils rewriting the extract through the eyes of Katie or Graham.

Plenary

Ask pupils to read out examples of the rewritten extract and encourage others to listen attentively. Comments from others should be invited on the successful elements of characterization and use of pronouns and proper nouns for clarity.

Assessment

Sentence level
Comment on the way pupils have used pronouns.

Writing composition
Ask pupils to comment on each others' reviews.

Model answers

Pupils' Book ⬚ A

1 *Three – Graham, Katie and the writer*
2 *Graham is shy with most people. The writer says so.*
3 *Katie is a bit of a show-off. She dances in the shop.*
4 *He's quite friendly.*
5 *She/he hates him.*

Pupils' Book ⬚ B

6 *I did not feel like breakfast.*
Not cornflakes and milk.
'Boring,' I said.

I made myself a jam sandwich.
'Yummy,' I said, rubbing my tummy.
I fed the teddy on my nightie, too.
NB – pupils may write 'thought' instead of 'said'.

⬚ 17A Connecting sentences ⬚

There will be some variations here; however, pupils should only use *Dinah* five times, and they should have used pronouns accurately.

This extract comes from the beginning of the story. It has been mistyped. The writer, Jacqueline Wilson, only used the name Dinah five times.

Work with a partner to swap *Dinah* for pronouns (*she, her, herself*).

The Dinosaur's Packed Lunch

Dinah woke up early.

Dinah didn't feel like getting washed. Dinah didn't feel like getting dressed. Dinah didn't feel like going to school.

'Boring,' said Dinah.

Dinah did not feel like breakfast.

Not cornflakes and milk.

'Boring,' said Dinah.

Dinah made Dinah a jam sandwich.

'Yummy,' said Dinah, rubbing Dinah's tummy.

Dinah fed the teddy on Dinah's nightie, too.

Jacqueline Wilson

1 Use a different colour for each character: Dinah, Judy, and the iguanodon. Starting with Dinah, highlight her name and every pronoun which is about her. Then do the other characters.

The Dinosaur's Packed Lunch

Everyone had a packed lunch except Dinah. Dad always forgot things like packed lunches. Sometimes Judy shared her packed lunch with Dinah. But not today.

'Ooh, my mum's given me prawn sandwiches and a bunch of grapes and a Kit Kat and a can of coke. Want half my Kit Kat, Danielle?' said Judy.

Dinah crept away, feeling very empty. She wandered back to the iguanodon, sucking her thumb.

'I wish I had a mum to make me a packed lunch,' said Dinah.

A hand reached out and patted her on the shoulder.

A huge scaly hand with a spiked thumb!

The iguanodon reached down and picked Dinah up. It cradled her in its arms, rocking backwards and forwards.

Extract from *The Dinosaur's Packed Lunch* (Doubleday, a division of Transworld Publishing, 1995), copyright © Jacqueline Wilson 1995, reprinted by permission of Transworld Publishers, a division of the Random House Group Ltd. All rights reserved.

2 Now list the pronouns used for each character:

Dinah	Judy	The iguanodon

17 *Personal pronouns*

All about pronouns

- Pronouns can be used in speech and writing to replace a noun or noun phrase. For example:

> *Dinah ate the sandwich. The **sandwich** was yummy.*
> *Dinah ate the sandwich. **It** was yummy.*

- Speakers and writers use pronouns to avoid repeating nouns again and again. This sounds clumsy. For example:

> *Dinah didn't feel like going to school.*
> *'Boring,' said Dinah.*
> *Dinah did not feel like breakfast.*

- Sometimes speakers and writers use too many pronouns. This can be confusing, because it is not clear who is doing what.

Using dialogue

The purpose of this unit is to encourage children to move beyond use of speech marks in punctuation of dialogue. Pupils will learn about standard English, and some basic aspects of grammatical agreement. They will also review the importance of dialogue in developing characters and illustrating their relationships.

NLS coverage

Key objective

SL 3 To ensure grammatical agreement in speech and writing of pronouns and verbs, e.g. *I am*, *we are*, in standard English
4 To use dialogue punctuation in writing; to use the conventions which mark boundaries between spoken words and the rest of the sentence

Learned through:

TL Reading comprehension
6 To compare forms or types of humour, e.g. by exploring, collecting and categorizing form or type of humour, e.g. joke poems, word play
7 To select, prepare, read aloud poetry that plays with language or entertains; to recognize rhyme, alliteration and other patterns of sound that create effects
8 To compare and contrast works by the same author
9 To discuss preferences and reasons for them

TL Writing composition
12 To write a first person account

WL 13 To collect synonyms which will be useful in writing dialogue, e.g. *shouted*, *cried*, *yelled*, *squealed*
16 To collect, investigate, classify common expressions from reading and own experience, e.g. ways of expressing surprise, apology, greeting, warning, thanking, refusing

Assessment criteria

SL By the end of this unit, pupils should be able to:
■ understand that there are different varieties/registers of English
■ recognize that standard English is the form in which we write
■ appreciate that there are specific rules which apply to standard English which may differ to their own spoken English, and that one aspect of this is agreement between pronouns and verbs
■ punctuate dialogue more effectively

WC Pupils should be able to write a 1st person account of a conversation

Session 1

You will need OHT 18, PCM 18A and PCM 18B.

Shared reading

1 Explain that in this session you will be reading two poems by Michael Rosen. He comes from Middlesex; he writes and performs poems for children as well as studying the English Language. Have any pupils heard of him? Introduce some poetry anthologies which contain his work, so that children can read it themselves at another time.

Ask pupils what sort of poems they expect: will they be sad, funny, descriptive? If they know Rosen's work, they may expect humour.

2 Tell the children that you are going to read and discuss each poem. You will then ask them what they think of each poem, and which they prefer.

Display and read *What's Your Name?* from OHT 18. Take pupils' initial responses in a brief discussion. Encourage them to articulate what they do or do not like about the poem.

- Do you like the poem? Simply that it's funny or silly would be enough
- Who do you think 'they' are in the poem?
- Why did Rosen use that? (i.e. 'They' – the adults – didn't think it was funny, but who might have done? – Rosen, his friends, his classmates?)

Now read the second poem from OHT 18 and take pupils' initial responses.

- Why does no one tell the grandfather that he snores?
- Discuss the repetition of *'did I snore?'*

3 Discuss which poem the pupils like best, and why. List the similarities between the poems on a chart:
- Both describe situations and behaviour which you might recognize.
- Both poems contain dialogue.
- They are similar in length.

Add any other features that pupils suggest. Ask what the differences are? Add these to the list. Summarize and explain that in the next session you will be reading another Michael Rosen poem.

Sentence level work

Draw pupils' attention to the dialogue and ask them to list the punctuation marks they notice in the poem. They should list capital letters, commas, question marks, apostrophes, and two different sorts of quotation marks. (See Unit 2 *Speech Punctuation* and Unit 14 *Commas*, if revision of the first three of these is necessary.)

Ask pupils to look at each punctuation mark and say what it is doing. Discuss full stops and capital letters and reinforce their function in demarcating sentences. Question marks should need little explanation!

Now consider the other punctuation marks:
- Apostrophe – represents parts of letters which have been omitted when two words are put together.
- Quotation mark – "Q". Rosen has used these because he could not have used speech marks within speech marks – i.e. it is already part of the dialogue.
- Comma – there are two types of commas in the first poem.

First, draw children's attention to the line
R,O,S,E,N

In this line, Rosen has put a comma between each letter to show us how to read it. Ask pupils what it would look like without commas: ROSEN. They might think he'd just written it in upper case, or he'd been shouting it! The commas tell them to name each letter.

Now look at the other places – in both poems – where commas have been used.

Before speech marks, there is a comma. Ask pupils to find examples of where this happens, maybe coming up to highlight each comma which is used in this way.

Independent activities

PCM 18A: *Punctuating the poem* offers pupils another Rosen poem – but without the speech punctuation. This will allow them to practise punctuation, and also to study another Rosen poem in some detail.

Abler pupils may need reminding about what to do when further speech occurs within speech. Less able pupils will need the early introduction of PCM 18B: *Comparing the speech punctuation* which provides a punctuated version of the poem.

Plenary

Compare PCM 18B – correctly punctuated version of the poem – with the one on which pupils have been working. Discuss any difficulties they encountered; remind children about the purpose of punctuation – to help the reader understand the flow of the dialogue easily.

Session 2

You will need Pupils' Book Unit 18 pages 40–41 and PCM 18B.

Shared reading

1 Introduce the Pupils' Book text as another poem by Michael Rosen. Remind children of the features of his poems from the last session, i.e. familiar situations, strong use of dialogue. Explain that you are going to ask them if the same features are present in this poem.

2 Read *I'm the Youngest in our House* in the Pupils' Book and take pupils' initial responses.
- Does this poem contain the same features as the other Rosen poems?
- Is there anything else that links the poems?
- How do you think the characters in the poem feel?
- Why does the narrator's brother begin this argument? (Might something specific have happened, or is this the way they are all the time?)
- How does the narrator feel at the end of the poem?
- Ask children to refer to their own experience – have you ever felt like this?

3 Focus on the way that Rosen uses the word *says* a lot in this poem. Look at the last verse, in particular. What alternatives are there to *says*? How has Rosen given other clues as to how the words are spoken in the words themselves, and the way in which he has

written them? (e.g. in capital letters – refer back to earlier part of the unit and see Unit 5 *Story verbs*.)

4 Explore the humour of the poem. Ask why it is funny. Pupils may feel it is funny because it reminds them of the way they argue with their brothers and sisters. Collect pupils' ideas for which is the funniest part. For example, in the end, the narrator cannot think of anything to say, so he says something silly.

Sentence level work

1 Examine the speech punctuation in *I'm the Youngest in our House*. Does it conform to the same rules as the poems from Session 1?

2 Remind pupils of earlier work on pronouns in Unit 17. Draw attention to the way they give us information. For example, how do we know that the voice of the poem is a boy? Children should be able to identify the pronouns that confirm this.

3 Now explain that you're going to look at grammatical agreement. Begin by talking about varieties of English. Draw attention to regional differences by comparing how English is spoken locally and in other parts of England and in other English-speaking countries. It may be useful to refer to a TV programme in which a different variety of English is spoken. Explain that there is one form of English, known as standard English, which is the same across the country. Anyone can understand it. It is also the form of English that is used in writing.

4 In standard English, there are rules. One of the main rules is about pronouns and verbs. If we are writing we need to make sure that if the nouns are plural the verbs are too. At this stage, you may wish to refer back to Unit 15 *Grammatical agreement*. However it would also be appropriate to model correct usage by taking some examples from the poem:

'Tell him to clear the fluff out from under his bed.'

translate this into a plural form:

'Tell them to clear the fluff out from under their beds.'

Draw pupils' attention to the way that the pronouns and nouns change together.
Now look at another sentence fragment, and do the same:

So now my brother – all puffed up – says...
So now my brothers – all puffed up – say...

What else has changed here? Notice the way that the verb changes when the subject of the sentence is changed. Experiment verbally with other extracts from the poem.

5 Take this opportunity to discuss the use of contractions in the poem: *I'm = I am* (pronoun + verb); *we're = we are* (pronoun + verb); *there's = there*

is (pronoun + verb). Some children may be able to see that *we're* is the plural form of *I'm*.

6 Discuss the way in which English is spoken locally and decide if there are any conflicts with the standard English of the poem. Ensure that pupils understand that there are rules which apply specifically to written English. The emphasis is not on changing spoken dialect forms, but on the need for standard forms in writing.

Independent activities

Activity A will help pupils to consider the relationship between the narrator and his brother in more detail.

Activity B is a sentence transformation task that will reinforce the discussion on grammatical agreement. Some sentences have been rewritten from the poem so that pronouns and verbs disagree. Pupils can use the poem to check their answers. The other sentences must be corrected from pupil's own understanding.

Plenary

Read the poem as a *readers' theatre*. Assign roles to specific children; others should comment on the effectiveness of their reading, taking into account expression and fluency.

Take feedback from pupils on their answers to activity B.

Session 3

You will need Pupils' Book Unit 18, pages 40–41 and the Reminder Sheet.

Shared writing

1 The purpose of this shared writing session is to allow children another opportunity to discuss the Rosen poems, and to write a non-chronological report. Your main focus will be modelling use of standard English in a writing context.

2 Reread *I'm the Youngest in our House*. Review whether or not pupils enjoyed the poem. Select some other poems by Michael Rosen with which they are familiar, and rank in order of popularity.

Write together

1 Explain that you are going to write a review about *I'm the Youngest in our House*.

Begin by reminding children about how you give information, in report form (see Unit 6 *Verbs in reports*). Discuss how this review might begin? (probably with an introduction about Michael

Rosen). Compose this together, remembering to model use of standard English, inviting children to complete phrases with the appropriate verb.

2 Move on to look at the pupils' favourite parts of the poem. Show how these may be included as quotations to illustrate a point. Take this opportunity to demonstrate use of speech marks where appropriate.

4 Review any parts of the poem that individuals did not enjoy and write about these.

5 Summarize the pupils' views on the poem in a final statement.

Independent writing activity

The shared writing should lead directly into activity C where pupils rewrite the argument from the brother's point of view. Explain that they will need to change the he/him pronouns to I/me. Ask them to write around 100 words. Distribute the Reminder Sheet, for support on speech punctuation and agreement, as needed.

Plenary

Share poems/accounts that come out of activity C. Discuss putting them together as an anthology. How might they be edited? Set up editing groups to work on the anthology. This may take place later in the term.

Assessment

Sentence level
All the pupils will be able to explain why we write using standard English.
Pupils should be able to correct non-standard English against a model text.
Pupils should also understand how to check their own work for noun-pronoun agreement.

Writing composition
Comment on the way in which pupils have drawn readers into the conflict between the brothers – have they elicted sympathy?

Model answers

Pupils' Book ⬡ A
1 *It only talks about two children.*
2 *Because his parents have backed him up. He is feeling self-important.*
3 *(Answers might include: bossy, snitching, annoying, bullying, stupid.)*

Pupils' Book ⬡ B
4 Here are some sentences which are not in standard English. Write them out correctly. The first four come from the poem, so you can use the text to check your answers.

My brother comes in and says:
So father says,
Now I'm angry.
YOU CAN'T RULE MY LIFE.

He likes apple pie.
They are not happy.
We are going home.

⬡ 18A Punctuating the poem ⬡
PCM 18B offers Rosen's original punctuation as a guide. Focus on the extent to which pupils have punctuated speech accurately. (The full stop at the end of the first line in the penultimate verse can be used as a discussion point.)

The speech punctuation is missing from this poem by Michael Rosen. Write in the correct speech punctuation to make it easier to read.

Rodge said,

Teachers – they want it all ways –

you're jumping up and down on a chair

or something

and they grab hold of you and say

Would you do that sort of thing in your own home?

So you say No.

And they say,

Well don't do it here then.

But if you say Yes, I do it at home.

they say

Well, we don't want that sort of thing

going on here

thank you very much.

Teachers – they get you all ways

Rodge said.

'Rodge Said', copyright © Michael Rosen 1979, from *You Tell Me: Poems by Roger McGough and Michael Rosen* (Kestrel, 1979) reprinted by permission of Penguin Books Ltd

Compare your version with Rosen's correctly punctuated poem.

> Rodge said,
>
> 'Teachers – they want it all ways –
>
> you're jumping up and down on a chair
>
> or something
>
> and they grab hold of you and say,
>
> "Would you do that sort of thing in your
>
> own home?"
>
>
> 'So you say, "No."
>
> And they say,
>
> "Well don't do it here then."
>
>
> 'But if you say, "Yes, I do it at home."
>
> they say,
>
> "Well, we don't want that sort of thing
>
> going on here
>
> thank you very much."
>
>
> 'Teachers – they get you all ways,'
>
> Rodge said.

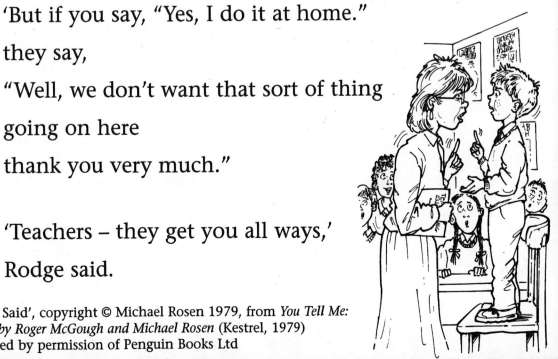

'Rodge Said', copyright © Michael Rosen 1979, from *You Tell Me:
Poems by Roger McGough and Michael Rosen* (Kestrel, 1979)
reprinted by permission of Penguin Books Ltd

Punctuating speech

It is important to use the right punctuation when writing dialogue, because it will make it much easier to read.
Here is some information to help you.

- The words that are actually spoken should be inside speech marks.

- A capital letter marks the beginning of a sentence.

- A comma separates items in a list or introduces dialogue.

- A question mark indicates that what went before is a question.

Grammatical agreement

The way we speak is often different from the way we write.
When we write we use standard English.
In standard English, there are rules. One of the main rules is about pronouns and verbs.
If you are writing, you need to make sure that if the nouns are plural the verbs are too. For example:

Tell him to clear the fluff out from under his bed.
Tell them to clear the fluff out from under their beds.

So now my brother – all puffed up – says...
So now my brothers – all puffed up – say...

Making longer sentences

The purpose of this unit is to allow pupils to explore a range of ways of expressing ideas clearly and succinctly by combining them in sentences. Pupils will also have opportunities to read from a range of dictionaries and glossaries as well as some other reference texts.

NLS coverage

Key objective

SL 5 To understand how sentences can be joined in more complex ways through a widening range of conjunctions in addition to *and* and *then*
7 To become aware of the use of commas in marking grammatical boundaries within sentences

Learned through:

TL **Reading comprehension**
17 To scan indexes, directories and IT sources, etc. to locate information quickly and accurately

TL **Writing composition**
24 To make alphabetically ordered texts – use information texts from other subjects, own experience
25 To revise and extend work on note-making
26 To summarize in writing the content of a passage or text and the main point it is making

WL 12 To collect new words from reading and work in other subjects, and use of them in reading and writing
15 To understand that some dictionaries provide further information about words, e.g. their origins, multiple meanings

Assessment criteria

SL By the end of this unit, pupils should be able to:
- identify a sentence
- identify a verb in a sentence
- use the present tense for writing reports
- divide a complex or compound sentence into two simple sentences
- combine two simple sentences into one complex sentence

TL **Writing composition**
Pupils should be able to write dictionary definitions of appropriate length and detail

Session 1

You will need OHT 19 and PCM 19A.

Shared reading

1 Begin by asking pupils what they do when they want to find out some information. They may suggest:
- Ask someone (parent/friend/teacher)
- Surf the Internet
- Use a book

All these are valid sources of reference for information of pupils who do not already know. Discuss the relative usefulness of these different sources: which is the quickest/most reliable/most fun/easiest?

2 Now look at how these sources are organized. Begin by talking about how you retrieve information from another person, i.e. it is necessary to ask the right question. It is not possible to check whether or not the information is *really* there.

What about the Internet? You still have to ask the right question. Search engines need you to use the right key words, for them to find the information you want.

Now turn to other reference materials – are they organized differently? Look at examples of dictionaries, glossaries, thesauruses, atlases, maps and encyclopedias. These are generally organized alphabetically or some variation on alphabetical order.

Display OHT 19: *Glossary of Materials* which supplies a number of glossary terms related to the Science topic: Materials.

Sentence level work

1   Referring to OHT 19, examine how the definitions are put together. Ask pupils if the glossary entries are written in sentences. Help them to identify the main parts of those sentences. They may notice that the sentences do not always begin with capital letters. Ask why might this be? Note that the word being defined does begin with a capital.

2   Discuss other ways of defining sentences, e.g. look for the full stops, counting the verbs. Look closely at the first definition:
Cotton comes from plants, and is used for clothing and fabrics.

This is one sentence; it has just one full stop. However, it has two verbs: *comes* and *is used*. Work with the children to break this down into separate sentences, for example:
Cotton comes from plants. It is used for clothing and fabrics.

Draw children's attention to the fact that each sentence has one verb. Ask them if there any other ways of writing this definition?

Look at where the writer has put a comma in the first sentence. It replaces the full stop and the deleted words.

Now look at the second definition:
Glass is made from sand. It is a hard, transparent material used for windows and mirrors.

The writer has used a comma between two adjectives – effectively a list of adjectives. Why does this definition not include another comma? Could it? Where would it go? Identify the appropriate place, using the previous definition as a model.
Glass is made from sand. It is a hard, transparent material. Glass is used for windows and mirrors.

Now compare the alternative definitions for *Cotton* and *Glass*. Which do pupils prefer – the original, or the divided ones?

Independent activities

Distribute PCM 19A: *Splitting up the sentences*. This allows pupils to practise breaking down the other definitions into more sentences.

Plenary

Encourage pupils to read back their own definitions. Look at variations, and discuss. Use this chance to reinforce points about how to identify sentence boundaries and the key elements of a sentence.

Session 2

You will need Pupils' Book Unit 19 pages 42–43 and PCM 19B.

Shared reading

1   The extract in the Pupils' Book is taken from the *Oxford Junior Dictionary*. Begin by asking children to look for specific entries: for example, who can be the quickest to read out the first word of the definition of *pure*.

2   Now make the task a bit more difficult! Ask pupils to find the word *cables*. This occurs in the definition of *pylon*: they will have to read and process the definitions in order to do this.

3   Discuss the advantages of alphabetical texts.

Sentence level work

1   In this session, work with pupils to combine sentences in the dictionary entries into longer sentences. For example, look at the definition of pylon. This can be broken down into two units:
a metal tower   *that holds up high electric cables*
description   extra detail

Consider other definitions and ask pupils if they follow the same pattern. For example, examine *pyjamas, pyramid, puzzle, quake*, etc.

2   Write some definitions for terms related to current topics. Use the sentence structure identified here: description, followed by additional detail.

Independent activities

Activity A in the Pupils' book encourages further scanning of the text for specific information, while activity B ask pupils to analyse the structure of individual entries as above.

PCM 19B: *Combining sentences* constitutes a simpler sentence combination activity for pupils who may struggle with activity B.

Plenary

Ask pupils to share their analysis of the definitions.

Discuss the results of PCM 19B and decide which sentences were the easiest to combine, and which had to be left. Compare with dictionary definitions.

Session 3

You will need Pupils' Book Unit 19 pages
42–43 and the Reminder Sheet.

Shared writing

1 Work together to develop a glossary for your current science topic. Generate a list of key words, and write each word onto a piece of card. Focus on nouns, as these have been the focus for the rest of the unit. For example, if you were working on *magnetism* you might select: *iron, copper, aluminium, magnet, pole, attraction, repulsion, string, plastic*

2 Remind the pupils of the features of definitions – particularly the way in which sentences are often joined together. Explain that for each key word you are going to collect lots of ideas first, then select from them, and finally work on the definition.

3 Select one of the key words and brainstorm as many ideas about the word as possible. Now, select the ideas that pupils think are most important, and would have to be included in a glossary.

Write together

1 Consider the audience for the glossary. Ask pupils if it is to be written for them. Or is it to be for others with no knowledge of it? Distribute the Reminder Sheet. Pupils should look first at which ideas go together. Then work on combining pairs of ideas into sentences to produce two or three definitions.

2 Remind pupils that definitions are written in the present tense. Experiment with different ways of combining ideas in sentences. Select the best version for each one.

3 Check on the punctuation, particularly the placement of commas. Try putting them in different places. Explain the reasons for the final position. If time, try combining some of the longer sentences.

Independent writing activity

Following on from the shared writing, pupils can work on definitions for the remaining key words. You may wish to work with a guided group on joining sentences.

Plenary

Encourage pupils to share their new definitions with the class and the sentence combinations in each one. Ask pupils to review the process they went through when writing definitions. Write up the process of writing definitions.

Assessment

Sentence level
Assess pupils' ability to manipulate sentences and sentence structures. They should be able to use the present tense consistently.
You will also have opportunities to observe pupils' understanding of verbs and verb phrases.

Writing composition
Invite pupils to work in pairs to see if they can identify the word from the definition. If not, discuss ways in which they could improve the definition. Have they used the structure offered in the Reminder Sheet?

Model answers

Pupils' Book ▱ A

1 (Check the appropriateness of pupils' rewording.)
2 *Power*
3 (Check use of the main features of the definition.)
4 *Between push and put*

Pupils' Book ▱ B

5 Word	Description	Detail
purr	to <u>make</u> the sound a cat makes	when it <u>is</u> pleased
purple	a colour	between red and blue

6 (Check pupils' other choices match the pattern.)

▱ 19A Splitting up sentences ⊒

Metal	*… They are often hard and shiny. Metals have many uses.*
Paper	*Paper is made from wood pulp. It is used for printing…*
Rubber	*… It is flexible. Rubber is used for insulation.*
Stone	*… Some stones are used for building. Some stones are valuable.*
Wood	*… Wood is used for buildings. It is used also used for furniture and fuel.*

▱ 19B Combining sentences ⊒

Drum	*A drum is a cylinder which you hit to make a booming sound.*
Guitar	*A guitar is a wooden instrument which has strings that you pluck.*
Piano	*A piano is a wooden instrument which has keys… .*

Splitting up sentences

Here are some definitions of different materials. Each definition has two sentences.

Rewrite each one in three or more sentences. The first one for *Glass* has been done for you.

Material	Definition
Glass	Glass is made from sand. It is a hard, transparent material used for windows and mirrors. *Glass is made from sand. It is a hard, transparent material.* *Glass is used for windows and mirrors.*
Metal	Metals are dug from the ground. They are often hard and shiny and have many uses. ....
Paper	Paper is made from wood pulp and used for printing. It can be dyed any colour. ....
Rubber	Rubber comes from rubber trees. It is very flexible, and used for insulation. ....
Stone	Stone is found everywhere on land. Some stones are used for building, some are valuable. ....
Wood	Wood is a natural material from trees. It is used for buildings, furniture and fuel. ....

Here is a page from a glossary of musical instruments.

1 Each definition has lots of short sentences. Can you put them together into one longer sentence? The first one has been done for you.

2 When you have finished, think of a title for your glossary.

Instrument	Definition
Cymbal	A cymbal is a large metal plate. You hit it to make a ringing sound. *A cymbal is a metal plate which you hit to make a ringing sound.*
Drum	A drum is a cylinder. You hit it to make a booming sound. ....
Guitar	A guitar is a wooden instrument. You pluck the strings. ....
Piano	A piano is a wooden instrument. You press the keys to play it. ....
Trumpet	A trumpet is a brass instrument. You blow it to make a sound. ....
Violin	A violin is a wooden instrument with strings. You play it with a bow. ....
Xylophone	A xylophone is an instrument with metal plates. You hit them with a stick. ....

Joining sentences

■ Every sentence has a subject and a verb. It starts with a capital letter and ends with a full stop. A sentence always makes sense.

■ Sometimes sentences can be joined together if they have the same subject. These joined sentences sometimes have more than one verb. For example:

> *I went home. I had my tea.*
>
> can become
>
> *I went home and had my tea.*

■ Writers can choose whether to write long or short sentences, depending on what they are writing.

Writing definitions

■ A definition is a statement of what a word means, or what a thing is.

■ A definition often has two parts, for example:

	Simple description	Extra detail
Pylon	*a metal tower*	*that holds up high electric cables*

■ Definitions are written in the present tense.

Pronouns & possessive pronouns

The purpose of this unit is to encourage pupils to use pronouns accurately and appropriately. Pupils will also read and write different sorts of letters.

NLS coverage

Key objective

[SL] 2 To identify pronouns and understand their functions in sentences through:
- distinguishing personal and possessive pronouns
- distinguishing the 1st, 2nd, 3rd person forms of pronouns
- investigating how pronouns are used to mark gender

Learned through:

[TL] **Reading comprehension**
3 To distinguish between 1st and 3rd person accounts
16 To read a range of letters; understand form and layout

[TL] **Writing composition**
12 To write a first person account
20 To write a range of letters and messages linked to other subjects
21 To use IT to bring letters to a published form
22 To experiment with recounting the same event in a variety of forms
23 To organize letters into simple paragraphs

[WL] 9 To recognize and spell the prefixes *mis-, non-, ex-, co-, anti-*
10 To use their knowledge of these prefixes to generate new words from root words

Assessment criteria

[SL] By the end of this unit, pupils should be able to:
- identify pronouns in sentences, and understand how they improve sentences.
- distinguish between different forms of pronouns, e.g. 1st/2nd/3rd person; personal/possessive
- understand how pronouns vary with number and gender

[TL] **Writing composition**
Pupils should be able to write a letter to entertain

Session 1

You will need OHT 20 and PCM 20A.

Shared reading

1 Prepare for reading OHT 20: *Dear Amy* by discussing the different sorts of letters that pupils might write or receive. Make a chart similar to the following:

We write to:	In order to:
friends	entertain
shop	complain

2 Display OHT 20: *Dear Amy* and read it through with the class, taking their initial responses.
- Which category does this letter fit into?

- What might be the relationship between Amy and Nicole?
- What clues are there about this in the letter?
- What else can we work out about them? – Are they the same age? Do they live near each other?

3 Discuss how Amy might feel on receiving this letter.

Sentence level work

1 Explain to pupils that there are different sorts of nouns in this letter. (Revisit Unit 8 *Using Nouns* if they need refreshing on this concept.) Begin by looking at common nouns. These are easy to spot: *letter, school, brother*, etc.

2 Review proper nouns with pupils through the names of all the individuals, the name of the month, and place names in the letter.

3 Explain that as well as these types of nouns, the letter contains pronouns which can take the place of nouns

or noun phrases in a sentence. Then work through this example from the text. Nicole has written:

We will probably go on holiday once Dad gets back from his trip.

She could have written:

Mum, Dad, Daniel and Nicole will probably go on holiday once Dad gets back from Dad's trip.

Ask why Nicole has chosen to use pronouns. Go through OHT 20 with the class, identifying and underlining the pronouns.

4 Experiment with replacing pronouns with nouns. Discuss the effects of this. Do pupils agree that pronouns make the letter read better?

5 Then try replacing all the nouns with pronouns. Encourage pupils to discuss why this does not work, i.e. it is difficult to follow who is doing what.

Independent activities

PCM 20A: *Using pronouns.* This invites pupils to read another type of letter – a letter of complaint that has been written without pronouns. The task is replace the nouns with appropriate pronouns.

Plenary

Discuss the letter from PCM 20A: *Using pronouns* with the class. Is it a good letter of complaint?

Review the pronouns that pupils have selected, checking that they all understand pronouns. Ask if anyone changed any other words? Most children will have changed the verb 'is' to 'am'.

Session 2

You will need Pupils' Book pages 44–45 and PCM 20B.

Shared reading

Before turning to *Dear Greenpeace* in the Pupils' Book, remind pupils that you read a letter (OHT 20: *Dear Amy*) in the last session. Explain that you are going to read two letters from a sequence called *Dear Greenpeace*.

1 Read both letters to the class. Ask pupils to comment upon the relationship between Emily and Greenpeace. What are their feelings about each other?

2 Reread the letters, this time with as little expression as possible. Ask children to comment on the two readings. How were they different?

3 Invite children to read parts of each letter with appropriate expression. Explore with them the words which they choose to emphasize and which make the difference to the reading.

Sentence level work

1 Revise the purpose of pronouns and ask children to identify pronouns in the letters.

2 Introduce pupils to the concept of *person*. Explain that Emily's letter is written in the *1st person*. That means that the writer is writing about something that happened to themselves. The pronouns tell us this. First person pronouns are: *I, me, us and we.*

In *3rd person* accounts the writer writes about things happening to another person. The pronouns they use are: *he, she, it, him, her, they, them.*

In the *2nd person*, the writer is writing to somebody and the pronoun used is *you.*

Ensure that pupils understand that these pronouns also apply in speech as well as writing.

3 Return to the letters and ask pupils to identify the first, second, and third person pronouns.

4 Explain that some of the pronouns are actually working as adjectives, for example in *your letter.* Using the word *your* saves Emily writing out Greenpeace again; it also describes the letter or gives more information about. *Your* is a possessive pronoun.

Pupils could be asked to brainstorm a list of other possessive pronouns, e.g. *my, their, our, her,* etc., and to find other examples from the letters.

Independent activities

Most pupils should be able to complete activities A and B in the Pupil's Book.

More able pupils could go on to PCM 20B: *Choosing the pronouns,* which allows them to investigate person and possessive pronouns further.

Plenary

Pupils who have completed PCM 20B: *Choosing the pronouns* can be invited to read out their completed letters. Ask the whole class if they can identify particular types of pronoun. This provides an opportunity for pupils to check that their answers are correct and for other class members to participate in work at this level.

Session 3

You will need Pupils' Book pages 44–45 and the Reminder Sheet.

Shared writing

Explain to pupils that you will now be writing a letter, this time to explain and apologize to a friend for not being able to get to his birthday party.

Remind pupils about how to set out a letter, using the previous shared texts as models, if necessary.

Write together

Begin by planning out the letter. How would you begin? Probably with an apology. You would then explain what had happened, and then apologize again. You might finish by saying when you were going to come around to give him his present.

As you write the letter, remind children that it is a serious letter. However, stress that when writing an apology you would probably try to gain someone's sympathy – so that they could see why you had let them down. This could be done by making the situation seem funny, or very sad.

Draw pupil's attention to the choices relating to use of nouns and pronouns and introduce the Reminder Sheet. Demonstrate why you have to be careful about using pronouns by over-using them until children notice, and then explain that it is difficult to trace the story. This is particularly useful if there are two characters of the same sex involved.

Edit for clarity once you have finished writing. Pupils should focus on the use of pronouns at this stage. They may also pick up other areas which could be clarified.

Independent writing activity

Following on from shared writing, pupils should complete activity C in the Pupils' Book. This offers children a plan for a letter written to entertain. Distribute the Reminder Sheet for support as needed in the use of pronouns and for letter writing.

Plenary

Invite pupils to read paragraphs from their own letters. Other class members comment upon what they liked about the letter. They may suggest one way of improving each letter.

Assessment

Sentence level
Check pupils' understanding of pronouns through completion of PCMs and Pupils' Book B activities.

Writing composition
These skills may not yet have transferred to pupils' writing. Accurate and appropriate use of pronouns in the writing task will be the next stage in development of this skill.

Model answers

Pupils' Book ⬜ A

1 *Emily is about 7 or 8.*

2 *Because she knows they know about whales*

3 *Take a photograph, contact the press, etc.*

4 *They think she's imagining it all. They say there is 'no way' a whale could live in the pond.*

Pupils' Book ⬜ B

5 *Last night Emily read Greenpeace's letter to Emily's whale. Afterwards the whale let Emily stroke the whale's head.*

6
Line	Possessive pronoun	Word(s) pronoun replaces
1	your	Greenpeace
2	my	Emily
3	his	the whale
3	your	Emily

⬜ 20A   Using pronouns ▣

Dear Mr Roberts

I am writing about some nappies I bought from your shop last week. They were for my grandson. The tape on the nappies did not stick well, and it often came undone in the night. The baby was left sleeping on wet sheets. I only used five of the nappies, as I was worried that he/she would be sore.

I used these nappies when my daughter was a baby, but I am very disappointed and I will not buy them from your shop again.

Yours sincerely

Andrea Dolley

⬜ 20B   Choosing the pronouns ▣

Thank you for the nappies you sent me. They are much better than the first packet. The baby has had no problems and I have been very happy to use these nappies on him/her at night.

I have told my family how kind you have been and I am sure they will use your shop now.

Yours sincerely

Andrea Dolley

20A Using pronouns

Read the letter below. It is a letter of complaint from Andrea to Mr Roberts who owns her local shop. Andrea has written this letter without pronouns. This does not make it easy to read.

Use an editor's red pencil to improve the letter by changing nouns to pronouns. You may need to change some other words too.

67 Summerbank Road
Robham

21 July 2000

Dear Mr Roberts,

Andrea is writing about some nappies Andrea bought from Roberts' shop last week. The nappies were for Andrea's grandson. The tape on the nappies did not stick well, and the tape often came undone in the night. The baby was left sleeping on wet sheets. Andrea only used five of the nappies, as Andrea was worried that the baby would be sore.

Andrea used these nappies when Andrea's daughter was a baby, but Andrea is very disappointed, and Andrea will not buy nappies from Roberts' shop again.

Yours sincerely,

Andrea Dolley

Choosing the pronouns

1 Mr Roberts has delivered some free nappies to Andrea. This is her letter thanking him for them. This time the pronouns have been left out. Write the correct pronouns into the gaps.

> 67 Summerbank Road
> Robham
>
> 26 July 2000
>
> Dear Mr Roberts,
>
> Thank .... for the nappies .... sent. ....
> .... are much better than the first packet. The baby has
> had no problems and .... have been very happy to use
> these nappies on .... at night.
>
> .... have told .... family how kind .... have
> been. .... am sure some of .... will use ....
> shop now.
>
> .... sincerely,
>
> **Andrea Dolley**

2 Look again at the pronouns in the letter and decide what type each one is. Then write each one into the right box in the table below.

	First person	Second person	Third person
Singular pronoun	I		
Plural pronoun	we		
Singular possessive pronoun			her / his / its
Plural possessive pronoun			

20 Pronouns & possessive pronouns

All about pronouns

- Pronouns can be used in speech and writing to replace a noun or noun phrase.

- Speakers and writers use pronouns to avoid repeating nouns again and again. This sounds clumsy. For example:

  Andrea is writing about some nappies Andrea bought from Roberts' shop last week.

- Sometimes speakers and writers use too many pronouns. This can be confusing, because it is not clear who is doing what.

  Andrea wrote to him about her grandson. She told him he had a really wet nappy in the night.

- There are different types of pronouns, depending on how many things they refer to, and whether they are male, female or neither.

Writing letters

- When writing letters, remember to include your address and the date of writing. You should finish the letter with a salutation.

- Remember that if you are writing to someone you do not know, you need to be very careful about grammar, punctuation, spelling, and handwriting. If you are writing a letter to a friend, you can relax a bit.